BARRY DIXON INTERIORS

BARRY DIXON

INTERIORS

BRIAN D. COLEMAN
PHOTOGRAPHY EDWARD ADDEO

GIBBS SMITH
TO ENRICH AND INSPIRE HUMANKIND
Salt Lake City | Charleston | Santa Fe | Santa Barbara

The author and photographer dedicate this book to their families and the
photographer wishes to remember David—E.A.

The author and photographer would like to thank the
homeowners for sharing their lovely residences for this book. ▪ This book would
not have been possible without the encouragement
and help of Barry Dixon's staff and we thank them all, especially Sue Wicks,
who was always there to take a call or answer another question. ▪
Barry and Michael's charisma and enthusiasm were the backbone of the project
and we will always remain deeply appreciative to both of them.

First Edition
1 2 3 4 5 6 7 8 9 10   08 09 10 11 12
Text © 2008 Brian D. Coleman
Photographs © 2008 Edward Addeo

Published by
Gibbs Smith
P.O. Box 667
Layton, Utah 84041

Orders: 1.800.835.4993
www.gibbs-smith.com

Designed by Debra McQuiston
Printed and bound in China

Library of Congress Cataloging-in-Publication Data

Coleman, Brian D.
Barry Dixon interiors / Brian D. Coleman ;
photographs by Edward Addeo. —
1st ed.
p. cm.
ISBN-13: 978-1-4236-0189-0
ISBN-10: 1-4236-0189-0
1. Dixon, Barry (Barry Darr)—Themes, motives,
2. Interior decoration—United States.
I. Addeo, Edward. II. Title.

NK2004.3.D59C65 2008
747.092—dc22
2007052836

CONTENTS

FOREWORD

How lucky for me that I arrived early for the opening night of the Southern Accents Showhouse in Virginia designed by Barry Dixon! He promptly swept me into his world and conducted an insider's tour of his creation. Never have I experienced such a complete immersion into a designer's mind and eye.

It was apparent to me, even before he spoke of his childhood as a global nomad, that real-life exposure to peoples and cultures worldwide was responsible for his refined international aesthetic. Having lived in Korea, Pakistan, India, New Caledonia and South Africa with his family, the world was literally his playground and school. Barry's father was a metals expert doing research globally, and very interested in teaching his family about the local history and traditions, while his mother's passion was for the indigenous natural beauty of the land and the crafts of the native population.

Experiencing such diverse lifestyles during his formative years enriched and heightened Barry's understanding of beauty and function. He experienced and embraced these special circumstances with an artist's sensitivity and a child's inquisitive mind. No surprise that Barry has retained memories of these exotic lands and incorporates his visions into magical interiors.

He often speaks of the many similarities that exist within humanity worldwide as a common thread that unites us all. The tapestry of life that Barry describes with great enthusiasm includes the master carvers, weavers, carpenters and others that he encountered and admired as a young boy—the perfect training ground for his future collaboration with the many trades people necessary to complete a job professionally.

The juxtaposition of antiques and new furnishings in his interiors seems natural and appropriate, as do the pieces that he designs for individual clients. A quirky table that caught my eye during that first meeting was a piece that he literally collaged together with parts salvaged from a favorite table in his grandparents' house, where he spent the summer. The glass ball accents and the metal feet were recycled and mixed with galvanized steel to create a unique accent table with great character and style.

One cannot forget another important ingredient that gives Barry's rooms warmth, functionality and soul. His Southern roots make being the perfect gentleman and host completely instinctive and appropriate. Knowledge of the historical past woven into the best of contemporary design and technology results in a body of work that is both timely and timeless.

This book takes the reader and viewer through private interiors that speak to the art of living in an original and believable manner. The inspiration and enjoyment from paging through these rooms should endure for generations to come.

—SHERRI DONGHIA
FORMER EXECUTIVE VICE PRESIDENT AND
CREATIVE DIRECTOR OF DONGHIA INTERNATIONAL

PREFACE

The ritual excitement of "setting up house" permeated my childhood. Born to parents whose curiosity and wanderlust spurred my father's longtime employment with an international metals firm, my younger sister and I may as well have been kidnapped by gypsies, as we hopscotched from one continent to the next on a magic-carpet ride of experiment and experience. Bratty kid that I was, I couldn't imagine how this worldly exposure to colors, cultures, regions and realms would shape my personal aesthetic point of view.

The flattering veil of memory edits the ordinary and focuses the sublime. Now we're sleeping under the thatched wonder of a rondavel in tropical French Polynesia, next we're opening our casement windows to astonishing views of the South African veld, fusing our southern American sensibilities and belongings (I was born in Memphis, Tennessee, after all) with a cacophony of international tricks and truths of everyday lifestyle. With each move and ultimate assimilation of the familiar with the exotic, I saw, lived and learned how to blend the seemingly disparate into a genial bespoke reality.

My personal path of interior enlightenment was littered with mini-epiphanies of what worked and what did not. (The logic of the illogical is sometimes hard to grasp.)

The staff of Barry Dixon Design gather on the landing at Elway (back to front, left to right): Michael Schmidt and Ellie, Teri Kreitzer, Barry Dixon, Danielle Wise, Rachel Brown, Kristine Weir, Laurel Mitchell, Danny Rodriguez, Jere Enloe, Nicole Rossetti, Sue Wicks, Cathy Foster, Catherine Proctor, and Dabney Doswell.

Somehow, blue seems to be a bad wall color in a frigid climate. And skirted beds (i.e., a good hiding place for critters) don't make for a good night's sleep in the tropics. Somewhere along the line it finally hit me that, simply put, balance was the key. Not so simple, and still being discovered, by me at least, are the elements that need balance: formal with informal, masculine with feminine, smooth with textured, shiny with matte, old with new, and on and on. The way we mix and stir these design ingredients determines the flavor of our interiors—and can certainly spice up our lives and the lives of those we care for in the process.

Our homes are our personal centers of the universe. They reflect our past, emanate our present and suggest our future. In the better instances, they intimate who we are—what we value, how we think—without giving away the whole secret, leaving enough mystery to romance a return. In the best instances, they transcend being about us to become about those we invite into our private world, their comforts, their imaginations and fascinations, their unspoken wants and wishes. Perhaps the greatest quality a home might possess is that of innate, soulful hospitality.

—Barry Dixon

INTRODUCTION

Barry Dixon Interiors began in 2005 when I first met Barry while we photographed his beautiful home for *Farrow & Ball: The Art of Color* (Gibbs Smith, 2007). I was fascinated and asked to see more examples of his work. Barry explained that his sense of style began during his childhood, which was spent in countries around the world. It was from this early exposure to a variety of cultures and designs that he developed an international approach, using classical architecture and traditional interiors along with elements of modern design to create elegant and very individual interiors. I was captivated and the idea of this book was born.

Organizing and photographing the book was certainly work but always enjoyable. We were able to visit a wide range of interiors around the country and abroad, from a breathtaking mountaintop villa in the sunny Caribbean to an eighteenth-century farmhouse in the rolling foothills of Virginia. We photographed a wonderful variety of Barry's designs: a powder room completely covered in seashells, a flat-screen television camouflaged behind a hinged screen of framed engravings, an open commons room for children carved out of an upper hallway recess.

Entrances create crucial first impressions, and Barry's are certainly spectacular: an arresting open staircase spiraling upwards in the form of a double helix; an inviting granite fireplace in a rustic Arts and Crafts foyer; thinly veiled linen scrims hung from the ceiling of a grand entry hall lending it intimacy and intrigue are a few of my favorites.

Barry's mastery of color is one of the keys to his success. Often drawing his inspiration from the local setting, Barry brings the colors found in nature to the indoors in these homes. A waterfront home in Florida had its dining room transformed into an undersea grotto with a hand-painted mural of the ocean deep in murky blues, turquoises and chartreuse greens, along with terrazzo floors hand mixed in sea green, sand, turquoise and raisin—colors of the ocean floor. In his own kitchen, the surrounding fields were brought inside with tiles in hues of hay, wheat and cream, while the beauty of mature oak trees in autumn was reinterpreted in another home's living room with a dreamy palette of sienna and smoky quartz, tobacco brown, taupe, cream and faded burnished gold. Barry explains how colors are crucial for the psychology of an interior; reds and golds, for example, are best to stimulate the appetite and promote conversation, while neutral creams and whites bring tranquility and invite one to relax.

Mixing old and new in fresh combinations is another of Barry's trademarks. A crusty terra-cotta capital reborn as a side table with the addition of a custom concrete top, a traditionally coffered ceiling inset with panels of raffia to better absorb sound, a very modern wire mesh parlor table that rests on classic glass ball-and-paw feet are some examples. Barry used a vivid sixties palette of hot pink and sunshine yellow in a guest bedroom in his Edwardian home, the bright hues giving the room's classic architecture a new and invigorating lease on life.

To help readers understand how Barry creates his interiors, we included some of his favorite design tips from each project, helpful advice such as placing a round rug in a square room to visually expand its perimeters, or turning eyesores into inspiration as in one home where exposed overhead pipes were repeated as ceiling curtain rods, successfully incorporating them into the overall design. Subtle repetition of elements throughout a room is key for cohesiveness and we demonstrate how Barry accomplishes this, for example, when a printed linen used for upholstery is repeated in a band edging the room's carpet.

Good design is important—it makes our environment more pleasing and pleasurable, balancing practical needs with aesthetics. It is my hope that by visiting this selection of interiors by Barry, readers will be inspired in their own projects and homes.

—BRIAN COLEMAN

MANHATTAN LOFT FOR ENTERTAINING

The entrance hall is the backbone of the loft. Its long corridor is subtly broken up by a horizontally striped runner from The Floor Gallery and curves of a brass table. A mesh tower made by Barry for Darr George (through J. Lambeth & Co.) holds an antique Cambodian earthenware jar. Walls, ceiling and mechanical systems are all painted in neutral Farrow & Ball "String."

SOON AFTER MOVING TO NEW YORK in the early 1990s, a major television producer fell in love with and purchased a quintessential Manhattan residence—a loft. Located in a late-nineteenth-century building in Tribeca, it was small—only 1,200 square feet—but had a desirable corner location. Wonderful light streamed through its large, one-and-one-half-story windows, and expansive views of bustling Manhattan streetscapes and even the Empire State Building uptown were classic.

The loft needed to be designed and decorated for frequent entertaining. So the owner called Barry, a childhood friend who had already designed two previous residences for him. As soon as Barry toured the loft, he knew his challenge was clear: make a small space function like something much larger—an apartment where one could have a hundred for cocktails at the drop of a hat yet also be intimate and inviting for day-to-day living.

Private quarters were kept to a minimum—just a master bedroom and bath, media center and guest alcove—while the public space was maximized by an open, flowing floor plan with areas that could be screened off into separate rooms by sheer overhead panels. As this was, after all, a loft, its function was not hidden but celebrated instead. Pipes, wiring and air-conditioning ductwork were purposefully kept exposed but carefully unified with one tonality of color: everything in the apartment was painted with off-white Farrow & Ball "String," except for punctuation marks of the kitchen and master bath. The pipes, in fact, were turned from eyesores into inspirations as the metal-rod motif was repeated overhead in ceiling-height drapery rods used to suspend the sheers.

The sixty-foot-long entry hall set the theme for the loft. Choreographed

Translucent sliding glass doors and an open ceiling make the master bedroom light and airy. Light reflects back into the small space through an "Eva" mirrored chest from Oly Studio in the corner and a mercury-glass chandelier overhead, which Barry designed for Darr George (through J. Lambeth & Co.) and which was inspired by a Lutyens design. The antique Moroccan chest is studded with bone, silver and ivory, FACING PAGE.

Original hide covers an antique table
in front of the living room sofa.

for guests and entertaining, the order of the rooms opening off it was carefully planned in an enfilade of function. Branching left, visitors first pass by a powder room to freshen up, then the master bedroom to leave coats and bags, followed by the kitchen and bar for drinks, and, finally, beyond the twenty-foot-tall diaphanous linen sheers into the dining and living spaces. To avoid seeming endless, the hall was foreshortened with subtle visual tricks—a brown and orange horizontally striped flat-woven-wool runner, along with a round brass accent table that, placed midway down the hall next to a window-seat ottoman, cleverly curves one's eye back toward the entry.

The master bedroom, just nine by ten feet, was kept open and inviting by the judicious interplay of light and vertical space. Translucent, ribbed sliding glass doors let daylight from the hall windows flood into the windowless room whose height was reinforced with an open ceiling and exposed pipes and ductwork. A mirrored chest of drawers from Oly Studio placed in the corner further expanded the small area by reflecting additional planes of light back into the room and adding much-needed storage. And still there was enough room for a king-size bed and upholstered headboard (custom designed by Barry), plus end tables. Since space is always at a premium in New York, a Pullman berth–style sleeping loft added above the closet at the other end of the room was a clever way to accommodate overnight guests.

Living in the center of Manhattan and surrounded by restaurants, the owner didn't need a large kitchen, so a simple galley was created. Open, lateral wooden shelves allowed an extra foot of visual depth. The small area was enlivened with a zesty Hermes-orange paint (Benjamin Moore "Bittersweet") to make the space seem less industrial and washing up less tedious. Exotic folk art accents—Balinese wooden bowls, a South African basket made from copper telephone

he galley kitchen opens off the hall past the bedroom. Stainless steel appliances are softened with Benjamin Moore rich and zesty "Bittersweet." Open shelves hold mementos and art from travels around the world. The entire space can be scrimmed off with drapery panels suspended from the ceiling.

A small media room behind the kitchen opens to the dressing room and master bath. A sleeping alcove is concealed above right. The walls are upholstered in soft gray Rogers & Goffigon mohair to absorb sound, and portieres from the same material substitute for closet doors. The "Love Ring" metallic sculpture on the right anchors the corner, FACING PAGE.

wire, a Moroccan carved box to hold tea—made the space more appealing when glimpsed down the long entry hall. A wheeled chrome cart with shelves and teak top for serving drinks helped separate the galley from the hallway.

A circular dining space adjacent to the kitchen was defined by a scrim of sheer curtains draped from the ceiling. Glamorous and sexy while still practical, the curtains can be opened or closed, layering and defining the space without the need for any walls. A round English Regency walnut dining table was placed in the center and lit overhead by an aubergine-and-amber-colored glass chandelier from Four Hands Company, that, strung on bronze wire, lent an industrial yet sophisticated charm. The dining room does double duty as a library, with a long, black, lacquered bookcase and storage unit along the back wall. An intimate media room was tucked behind, its walls upholstered in warm mouse-gray Rogers & Goffigon mohair velvet accented with a bronze metallic nail-head trim.

Because the loft boasts two large side windows overlooking the Empire State Building, maximizing the living room's view was crucial. Barry reinforced the vista with a vertical mirrored screen placed against the opposite wall to reflect the city back into the room; its smoky, wavy panes of glass add a romantic, otherworldly appeal, and its very design is an abstraction of the buildings in the cityscape. An eighteenth-century Irish carved-oak console placed in front of the mir-

rored screen functions as a contrast, its gentle curves softening the screen's hard-lined, industrial grids. To anchor the room, an eleven-foot-long Christian Liagre "La Toja" sofa in "Agora," a creamy silk-linen Bergamo blend, was placed beneath the windows, while other furniture was kept moveable to accommodate large parties—a classic Eames-style circular table in bittersweet orange, along with an easily portable "Roseanne" chair, a design of Barry's that features a sculptural, see-through trefoil back. Bergamo "Grazia," a cotton-and-silk blend, was used for a pillow whose stylized, embroidered silk detailing hints an Arts and Crafts sensibility. The elements of nature were emphasized with a cluster of sunset-colored glassware, an amber Murano glass orb, an antique peachblow decanter and an organic Donghia cylinder of translucent gold—grouped on top of a table from Botswana made from a tripod of spiraled kudu antelope horns. Window treatments were kept straightforward with translucent, handwoven-natural-fiber Conrad shades and unlined panels of Henry Calvin linen sheers from Donghia.

This small urban loft has managed to combine three separate sleeping spaces, two baths, a kitchen, laundry, functioning study-library and dining room, generous living room and separate foyer and hall in just over 1,000 square feet. With good planning and design, Barry accomplished everything the owner desired, creating a sleek, sophisticated yet functional apartment for both entertaining and everyday living.

A GRID OF WAVY GLASS SQUARES SET INTO A SCREEN REFLECTS

light into the living room; designed by Barry for Darr George (through J. Lambeth & Co.). Each glass panel was
handblown, then silvered and washed for a murky, underwater effect. A softly curved antique
Irish console softens the space; cast-bronze pigeons alighted on the salvaged balustrade are an allegory of the city, *above*. ▪
The dining room is centered on an antique English Regency circular table with upholstered chairs
from Julian Chichester. The freestanding mirrored screen against the far wall makes the room seem larger. Floors
throughout the loft wear their original walnut finish, *facing*.

*T*he tower of the Empire State Building is echoed in the shapes of sunset-colored Murano glassware grouped on a wooden-topped table from Botswana. The Murano glass Donghia floor lamp adds to the sparkle and shine, *facing*. ▪ Sammy supervises activity in the living room from the "La Toja" sofa from Christian Liagre covered in Bergamo "Agora" silk-and-linen blend. The bittersweet-orange Eames-style table complements the orange-and-tan embroidered Arts and Crafts pillow from Sacho Hesslein, *right*.

Barry's Tips

▪ Don't be afraid of mechanical elements and turn them from eyesores into inspirations—pipes and ductwork can be left exposed and repeated in details such as curtain rods.

▪ Boomerang the eye back down a long, narrow hall with round accents—occasional tables, ottomans, lamp shades or art.

▪ If you live in the city bring urban materials back inside with glass, iron, stone and brick.

▪ Mirrored furniture disappears and appears to take up less space in tight quarters.

▪ Make a simple galley kitchen more exciting with bright color, artwork and collectibles.

NEW
AND OLD
ON THE
POTOMAC

A subtle juxtaposition of designs is what lends the soaring living room its character—geometric grids and lines played against circles and curves; cool industrial materials against warm earth-toned fabrics. The primitive cocktail table is wengewood from Christian Liagre. A Tomlinson club chair in the foreground wears orange textured linen and wool from Bergamo.

BUILT ALONGSIDE THE Potomac River, this newly constructed home aptly reflects the owners' personalities—eclectic and down-to-earth, mixing classic and modern, new and old. Barry and the owners began by traveling together on buying trips across the country and to Europe; for two years they attended antique shows in New York and Washington, shopped in London over Christmas, and traveled the countryside of France and Italy searching for just the right furnishings. The time they spent together had an additional advantage: Barry got to know the owners better and found it easier to draw out nuances of their personalities and subtly inject them back into his designs for their home.

The lady of the house is a performing singer who loves a dramatic entrance. So, an arresting, sweeping staircase in the form of a double helix was spiraled just beyond the foyer. A system of connecting grids was designed as the railing, its geometric wrought-iron squares boldly outlined against the curve of the stringer and a tall bank of windows on the far wall granting views of the sparkling Potomac River just beyond. Cast-plaster beams faux finished as limed oak and supported by hand-cast metal straps crown the stairwell ceiling. The plaster walls were faux painted in a "deconstructed" finish palette of warm Tuscan colors—terra-cotta and pale gold glazes layered over Benjamin Moore "Linen White." Carpeted with a straightforward sea grass runner, the drama of the stairs continues down to the last tread, where the runner ends with a fanfare of a flared fish tail. A vortex of movement and space, the staircase visually binds the home's three levels together.

The adjacent dining room continues the Tuscan palette with silvery gold-and-peach silk Fortuny "Solimina" draperies and adobe orange walls,

The intimate library beckons *through French doors* off the entry. The walls are painted with Farrow & Ball "Wainscot" and a vintage parchment shade hangs from the ceiling over the library table. The globe is eighteenth century; the antique iron bookstand was found in France, FACING PAGE.

inspired by summer sojourns in Florence and Siena. A watery, mirrored screen reflects glimpses of the garden from across the room, while a rare seventeenth-century Portuguese carved table rests in front. Mid-nineteenth-century Italian side chairs with their original leather seats flank the dining table, and the old-world atmosphere is further reinforced with a pair of Carrera marble urns on the dining table and a delightfully crusty Roman stone bust from a garden in front of the mirrored screen. Lit by overhead glass bell jar lanterns designed by Barry and delicate antique wrought-iron wall sconces, the room is dreamy and romantic, an ode to candlelit suppers amongst the olive groves.

Across the foyer and adjacent to the music room, a gentleman's library was added, its small size subtly camouflaged with a circular sea grass carpet. An octagonal, coffered plaster ceiling lends the room both instant intimacy and grandeur. Chocolate gauffraged velvet drapery panels ("Mazarin" from Quadrille) at the windows absorb sound and add to the coziness, while a pair of lolling chairs conjures an Edwardian gentleman's club. The ample library table was actually the dining table in the owners' previous home. A parchment shade was hung above the table to provide light, keeping the desktop open, with enough space for reading, correspondence or a game of backgammon.

The nubby sea grass center rug is banded with a two-inch border of "Fata," a woven velvet from Zimmer & Rhode.

The drama of the home is continued in the twenty-four-foot-tall family room. Unconventional yet urbane, it is centered on a two-story fireplace wall of large concrete grids that echo those of the stair rails and skillfully conceal television and other media equipment behind. As the owners are voracious readers, industrial steel bookshelves were set in bronze tracks across the back of the room, at once expandable for seating and reading or collapsible when more space for entertaining is desired. The power of geometry—straight-lined grids and squares played against circles and curves—was used to give the large room movement and interest in a mix of architectural salvage: a 1930s circular clock face salvaged from a Philadelphia bank building centered against the grid of the fireplace, and a collage of large, machine gears hung on the opposite wall. A naïve yet powerful wooden sculpture from Cameroon repeats the interplay of circles and squares near the front of the fireplace, while the horizontal lines of the steel bookcases organize space across the room.

Warm, organic colors were chosen to soften the industrial elements: a mid-century modern "Frank" sofa from Stewart was upholstered in a ribbed, orange cotton-and-linen blend from Sacho Hesslein and accented with citrus-and-pumpkin-orange-striped velvet pillows from Old World Weavers (the

The downstairs guest bedroom is *centered on a headboard* of cubicles painted in bright "Startling Orange" from Benjamin Moore. The bed cover is a warm gold chenille, FACING PAGE.

fabric is also on the seats of a pair of vintage garden chairs). A 1930s Moderne chair found in Paris was upholstered with an Osborne & Little herringbone-striped printed linen; the fabric was repeated in two-inch banding around the edge of the room's sea grass area rug whose bold linear pattern subtly defies the irregular perimeters of the room.

The kitchen is the owners' favorite spot to relax, so enough space was allocated for a generous and welcoming room but with intimate areas—a fireplace nook, a curved banquette along the outer wall with views of the gardens and the rushing falls of the river. Contrasts were deliberately employed to give the room more power and excitement—the light from silvery galvanized steel countertops anchored with large brass studs bounces off the creamy Pratt and Larson backsplash tiles and a cast-stone hood above the stove, as well as the stone mantel across the room.

Geometric allegories were not forgotten: kitchen cabinets were designed with a Celtic circle-and-cross motif reminiscent of the work of the famous Scottish Arts and Crafts designer Charles Rennie MacIntosh of the early twentieth century. Cabinets were covered with a translucent wire mesh for extra visual depth yet still with some veiling (contents are not as obvious as with clear glass panes) and stained with translucent olive-green aniline dye inspired by the faded tones of early-nineteenth-century French enamelware. The favorite spot for a romantic dinner for two is in front of the fireplace, nestled in a pair of tall "Bretonne" wing chairs from Niermann Weeks. The chairs were covered in a textured cotton-and-linen blend from Rubelli, its pattern a swirl of quatrefoils that are repeated on the cast-

stone mantel. Colors in the kitchen are appropriately drawn from the land—yellow-green onions and artichokes—and translated to the hand-colored, textured plaster walls.

The master suite upstairs was conceived as an airy retreat. Set at the highest point in the house, its walls were painted with Farrow & Ball wistful blue "Borrowed Light." Circles and squares were continued with the square bedroom opening to the circular sitting room set in a rounded turret and an elegant, sparkling silver-and-glass master bath. Space was cleverly expanded by cutting out the ceiling above the bed and adding twelve inches, to suspend bed curtains overhead and to allow space for a fan, creating the illusion of a canopy where there was none. "Ah-net" platinum silk wool from Pollack was chosen for the outer bed curtains, while the interior panels and coverlet were fashioned from Rubelli creamy silk "Venus." Masculine and feminine elements were subtly juxtaposed for a pleasing reference to the husband and wife occupants—rough wool against soft silk bed hangings, a sensual silver-and-mirrored vanity in the master bath against a primitive Victorian wood-slatted bathing screen.

The lower level of the house was designed for guests and privacy. An eye-catching, salvaged breakfront of octagonal and square niches was reborn as a headboard, its classic, Jeffersonian-like design repeated as a combination footboard and room screen. Painted in "Startling Orange" from Benjamin Moore and "India Yellow" from Farrow & Ball, the bed sings a song of welcome for its guests.

Witty, eclectic and very personal, this home brims with the warmth of its owners.

A bank of windows overlooking the Potomac River lights the stairwell. The two-story living room is anchored by a grid of concrete panels above the fireplace, six faux finished in Masonite to conceal media equipment. An antique garden lattice partially screens the living room from the foyer, *above.* ▪ Osborne & Little's primitive herringbone-printed linen covers a chair as well as defines the perimeter of the living room, reinforcing the play of geometric lines and patterns, *left.* ▪ A comfortable corner of the living room nestles around a curved Normandy banquette designed by Barry and a circular center table by Christian Liagre. Curtain panels of "Douglas" linen from Henry Calvin add to the intimacy and softly filter the afternoon sun. The overhead cylindrical mesh lantern was designed by Barry; curved pieces in a corner help guide the eye back out into the room, *facing.*

The double helix staircase swirls down three stories to the core of the house and ends in a pit of pea gravel set with a stone garden table and stools, *left*. ▪ The sea grass carpet runner ends in a decorative fish tail that spills out onto the coffee bean–colored concrete floor (a handful of coffee beans was Barry's inspiration), *below*.

OVERLEAF: The dining room glimmers with reflected lights in a mirrored screen set in front of an eighteenth-century Portuguese carved side table. The burled pearwood dining table is from New Classics. The foyer beyond was painted in five twenty-inch-wide horizontal bands of butter cream and vanilla alternating with burnt orange and saffron and centered with a "Nettie Darr" steel mesh table designed by Barry for Mike Reid Weeks.

A gently curving breakfast bar divides the kitchen into semicircles for cooking, eating and entertaining. Patterns and textures, steel and metal, wood, stone and tile all play against each other for subtle and pleasing visual interest. Antique olive green bottles on the counter highlight the room's palette. An overscaled iron chandelier balances the banquette and adds a note of drama, *below.* ▪ Wire mesh cabinet fronts conceal the contents yet add more visual depth to the Arts and Crafts–inspired cabinets. Aniline green stain was inspired by vintage French enamelware, *above facing.* ▪ A cabinet detail shows the interplay of textures and surfaces. Cabinet pulls (actually front

door handles from LV Brass) turned sideways are just the right length for hanging dish towels. Galvanized steel countertops are impervious to moisture and stains, *middle*. ▪ A stone hearth across the room is a cozy spot for dinner. Andirons from Lyle and Umbach are designed to warm bowls of porridge by the fire. The textured plaster walls were hand painted in warm mustard yellow and ochre stains. Hand-forged iron wall sconces are from Dennis & Leen, *below*.

THE MASTER BEDROOM is centered on a faux-canopied bed whose drapery is actually suspended from an inset in the ceiling. The bed coverlet is "Venus," an embroidered Rubelli silk, whose creamy tones are continued in the silk Pollack & Associates bed hangings. Chairs in front of the stone mantel are Baker Knapp & Tubbs, *facing*. ▪ A sparkling Waterford crystal candelabrum enhances romantic soaks in the tub. The rolling wooden bathing screen behind the tub provides an unexpected Victorian touch, *left*. ▪ A circular sitting room in the turret adjoins the master bedroom, *below*.

Barry's Tips

- Visually expand or camouflage the perimeter of a square room with a circular carpet.

- Use repetition of basic geometric shapes—circles, squares and diamonds—as a tool to link different elements in a room.

- If you are color shy introduce a bold color in areas not in daily use—a formal dining or living room, or guest room.

- Hang a lamp over a desk to give more tabletop space and keep the surface uncluttered.

- Wire mesh in a cabinet gives light and visual depth but allows the contents to remain obscured.

OLD-WORLD CHARM IN
CHEVY CHASE

A corner of the living room beckons with an exotic charm with Barry's "Odalisque" sofa upholstered in Donghia silk and a tufted "Dana" ottoman covered in Bergamo "Venus," a pearl-colored silk-and-cotton blend. Gilded Venetian Doges chairs are slipcovered with "Kenia" from Aviron Textiles.

WHEN THE OWNERS OF this elegant, 20,000-square-foot home in Chevy Chase contacted Barry, they had just begun planning it. Unable to find exactly what they wanted, they had purchased three acres in a leafy Washington neighborhood and torn down the existing structures, diligently preserving the mature oak trees on the property. As the family makes frequent Continental sojourns, they requested something classic, by necessity built from the ground up but with old-world patina and sophistication.

Barry began by poring over the blueprints with the architect and owners, deconstructing large rooms into more intimate spaces and adding visual interest—curved walls, generous conversation areas in the upper halls, a barrel-vaulted ceiling in the dining room inspired by a Lutyens Arts and Crafts country house in England. Soon a sophisticated structure began to emerge, for all appearances an old and distinguished grande dame that might have gracefully evolved over time.

The exterior was built of stone and its influence continued indoors to the entry hall in the form of paved limestone floors and textured plaster walls faux finished in Benjamin Moore's "Linen White," with an amber wash for an impression of old but warm stonework. A pair of eighteenth-century Swedish settees (one original, the other an exact replica) were chosen to center the space and upholstered in Quadrille's cocoa-and-cream silk brocade "Venezia," to complement the mineral tonalities of the room. Crusty, carved limestone garden urns were placed on either side of the massive, hand-carved walnut front door, much like an ancient French chateau. The husband enjoys hunting, so an allegory to the sport was made with four bronze-and-iron wall sconces, each decorated with a set of

A seventeenth-century gilded and heavily carved English cabinet from Randall Tysinger anchors the corner. A collection of nineteenth-century Italian intaglios hangs on the wall— souvenirs, perhaps, of a Grand Tour. The walls are painted in a mural of foggy dreamy woodlands using colors from the room's furnishings, *above left.* The "Dana" ottoman was decorated with nail-

head trim in a floral design reminiscent of the murals. The composition stone fireplace holds a collection of antiques: a pair of architectural masks found in Paris, amber Czechoslovakian candlesticks, a sixteenth-century Italian oil of a mother and children, *below facing*. ▪ The entry hall is centered on a round iron table topped with an antiqued mirror. The three-armed iron chandelier repeats the table's curves overhead. The limestone floor was hand chiseled for the look of an ancient French chateau. Doors on either side of the entry lead to oval alcoves with window seats, *above*.

THE FOYER LEADS to the exotic and alluring living room built upon a mélange of architectural elements—Egyptian columns, a custom plaster ceiling, hand-painted wall murals. A pair of Tomlinson "Patricia" slipper chairs in "Venus," a silk and cotton blend from Bergamo, flank a long "Palermo" Knoll sofa from Panache. The leather four-paneled screen is Dutch, c. 1870. The sea grass carpet is bordered with "Topkapi," a woven tapestry border from Gisbert Rentmeister.

gilded horns. And to help alleviate angularity, a pair of oval domed rotundas were added flanking the front door, each with an inviting window seat overlooking the front gardens and cobblestone drive.

The foyer leads directly into the central axis of the house. To the right are broad stairs that ascend to the second-floor bedroom suites; to the left are the dining room, kitchen and family quarters overlooking the pool and rear gardens; straight ahead, through stately Egyptian-inspired pilasters, is the living room; and beyond it is the formal library and study.

The living room's walls were cloaked in an ethereal, hand-painted mural of misty branches and leaves that bathe the room in a smoky, dreamlike haze. The mural was deliberately muted as to not dominate the decor, its palette of sienna and smoky quartz, tobacco brown, taupe, cream and faded burnished gold pulled from the furnishings of the room. A modestly scaled stone fireplace centered the far wall and was pleasingly contrasted with a gilded seventeenth-century English cabinet anchoring the adjacent corner, its classic arches, pilasters and intaglios referenced in the geometric design of the plaster ceiling overhead. A romantic note was suggested with Barry's curved-back "Odelisque" sofa, which was covered in Donghia "Bindi," an embossed silk in creamy almond; the fabric's Hindu designs were complemented by a pair of antique Moroccan lidded urns resting on the English cabinet behind. Baroque influences were evoked with a pair of Venetian Doges chairs flanking a tufted "Dana" ottoman with bun feet and decorative nail-head trim. Campaign-style Fortuny draperies of "Vivaldi" cotton in Rembrandt rust, straw and silvery gold flank the windows on either side of the fireplace and hang from custom hand-hammered wrought-iron drapery rods of trailing leaves and vines that extend the wall murals to the window tops. A nineteenth-century leather Dutch screen anchors the opposite wall, its gilded and embossed tooling glinting in subdued light. A 160-inch-long overstuffed settee rests in front of the screen, each corner lit by one of a pair of sparkling nineteenth-century mercury glass

Circular ceiling designs cleverly break the rectangular study into two spaces: the foreground for sitting and reading, the rear for dining and games. A chocolate brown–and–persimmon Tibetan wool rug anchors the room, while sculptural, seven-foot-tall, fin-de-siècle bronze floor lamps illuminate the desk and sofa. An embossed English leather screen, c. 1860, helps divide the areas, FACING PAGE.

table lamps found in Paris. Alluring and dreamy, the room is an exotic pastiche of ingredients for enjoyable entertaining.

Beyond the living room, the handsome library was designed as a masculine retreat for the gentleman of the house. A curving staircase at the rear descends to the extensive wine cellars below. Limed oak–paneled walls and custom-designed bookcases were highlighted beneath a ceiling of overlapping plaster circles of oak leaves. The design invokes hemispheres of ancient mariners' maps.

As stimulating to the eye as to the appetite, the dining room is richly upholstered in a colorful Robert Kime printed linen, which also acts to discretely absorb the clatter of dining. A handsome barrel-vaulted ceiling inspired by a Lutyens English country house envelops the room in its embrace, while a pair of eighteenth-century Italian gilt bronze chandeliers provide an elegant glow. Vermillion-colored George Smith settees on either side of the fireplace were paired with two early-nineteenth-century Venetian fauteuils to create cozy corners for afternoon tea as well as additional dining space. A built-in banquette nestled into a niche in the hallway opposite was upholstered in ecru linen damask from Old World Weavers to break up the long passage. While warm and intimate, the dining room can nonetheless hold up to fifty for dinner, seating guests at the tea tables and banquette as well as the main table—a handsome straight-grained walnut and pear wood double pedestal designed by Barry for the room.

Past the dining room, the kitchen, breakfast and family room triptych is the heart of the home. More modern than the formal reception areas, these rooms were designed to be light and open, with a limed oak beamed ceiling inset with straw-colored raffia panels to absorb sound. Warm and sunny colors were chosen and the curtains fashioned in citrus Donghia fabric. Walls were painted with Benjamin Moore's "Misty Air," exuding the romance of foggy morning light, and complemented with a hand-woven Ti-

betan carpet in tones of melon, gold and vernal green. A central ottoman was designed with a quilted mattress top that makes a great spot for lounging, watching television or playing checkers. The light graining of a pair of pear wood trestle tables in front of the sofa echoes the ceiling beams. The television is cleverly concealed behind a screen of nineteenth-century engravings of eggs—a motif repeated in a collection of ostrich-egg-sized river stones collected from the Indus River in India that rest serenely in an earthen bowl.

As the husband likes to cook, a masculine kitchen was created, a fairy-tale scullery of cobblestone floors, farmhouse sinks, bronze tiles and gleaming copper pots. The room was divided into four task areas, each with its own sink and workstation: food prep, drinks and bar, clean up and all-purpose. Industrial machine-age designs abound: hammered bronze tiles set with square rivets behind the stove and a forged, custom hood with bronze and copper fittings above; countertops constructed from hand-hammered iron with copper studs. A breakfast bar helps separate the cooking and preparation areas but still leaves the room open for conversation. "Bachelor's Button," a custom hand-blocked Morris paper in coppery gold, covers the ceiling, which is punctuated with a trio of hanging conical copper lights.

Upstairs, attention to family living space was continued with a large and welcoming upper mezzanine that doubles as a conversation and communal gathering area. The concept of a gallery was extended from the stairwell, and the walls were hung with collections of art and sculpture, among which are six hand-colored engravings by Czechoslovakian artist Jiri Anderle grouped together as one large piece of art, magnifying their strength and visual impact. A nineteenth-century French carved-walnut hunt table with an Italian marble top centered the landing, and comfortable seating

continued on page 55

A late-nineteenth-century Turkish Oushak carpet in brilliant coral, gold and celadon green sets the color palette for the dining room, whose walls are upholstered in Robert Kime's exuberant "Tree of Life." A pair of George Smith settees adds extra dining space by the fireplace. The dining table and chairs (designed by Barry) are a fusion of traditional Queen Anne and Italian influences, *left*. Tea is often taken at the coral linen velvet settees and Rose Tarlow gilt branch side tables. Note the burnished brass tacks, which give the upholstered walls a more finished and tailored look, *below*.

The long passage leading from the entry through the dining room to the breakfast room beyond is broken up with a button-tufted, built-in banquette that provides extra seating for large dinner parties. Walls are upholstered in Old World Weavers "Katmandu" damask. Red and gold Fortuny pillows are warm accents. The breakfast room is centered on a table

made from Stoneyard's cast-limestone base designed from a fourteenth-century stone well, *below left*. ▪ The open and sunny family room adjacent to the breakfast room is a favorite spot for all of the family. Seating is comfortable and low key: a pair of Tomlinson's "Boomerang" upholstered lounge chairs flank a comfortable "Marche" sofa, while a Formations ottoman in the center is versatile for both lounging and games. Limed oak ceiling beams add a handcrafted Arts and Crafts appeal, *below right*.

A television screen made from framed nineteenth-century engravings from Avery Fine Art conceals the television when not in use. Organic influences, including a root wood bowl on the walnut console table, river stones from the Indus River and Moroccan amber beads in a primitive wooden bowl on the ottoman add a note of serenity, FACING PAGE.

was loosely grouped about—including a pair of velvet Rose Tarlow "Sophia" chairs and a Regency settee with its original mustard-yellow tufted-leather upholstery still intact.

Directly beyond the upper mezzanine, the master suite begins with his and her baths, dressing rooms and vestibules converging onto the master bedroom. Her bath was conceived as a romantic, otherworldly Venetian grotto, with mosaic stone floors continuing several feet up the wall, as in a Roman bath, and capped with a border of sea blue and green mosaic glass tiles for an undersea effect. Finished with Venetian plaster, the walls were impregnated with ground marble dust and painted with aqua blue Farrow & Ball "Borrowed Light," and then polished with seven coats of beeswax, for a deep, watery sheen. The ceiling was arched and outlined with ribs made from plaster casts of real seashells, reminiscent of a ship's hull. An old-fashioned claw-foot tub from Waterworks was installed in front of the cast-stone fireplace—perfect for long, relaxing soaks in front of a roaring fire. Accessories, including a pair of large turquoise spice urns found in Marrakech to hold bath salts, oversized South Sea clamshells and a Venetian glass lantern overhead, lend to the atmosphere of an exotic undersea grotto.

The children's suites reflect the personalities of their inhabitants. A Bohemian-chic bedroom and bathroom to match were designed for the teenage daughter, who loves everything pink. Thus, glass mosaic tiles in three different shades of her favorite color were chosen—lilac, salmon, and hot pink—and installed in a random pattern. A cap of colorful crenellated ceramic tiles from Pratt and Larson was added above to suggest the exotic air of an Alhambra (palace of the Moorish monarchs). An Edwardian-style cast-iron tub from Waterworks was placed for period

appeal (cast iron holds the temperature of hot water longer), with its sides given a creamy, faux stone finish. Walls were painted in tropical pink Benjamin Moore "Fruit Shake," and pink accessories were chosen: blown pink glass vials for bath salts, a pretty pink Eames tabouret and delicate pink Chinese garden seats. Window shades were made from Osborne and Little "Azin" silk, whose long, vertical lines of dots could seem much like curving trails of bubbles from a fanciful sea creature; the irregular base of the shade imitates the curves of a wave.

The younger daughter's bedroom was kept delicate and feminine, befitting its dainty occupant. The ceiling was painted in Farrow & Ball "Cooking Apple Green" and the walls were upholstered in pretty pink hand-blocked linen "Ceylon Borscht" from Raoul Textiles and finished with piping at the corners. Window treatments were fashioned in coordinating "Cameo Borscht," with elegant, ruffled, box-pleated valances whose classic and timeless design was meant to stay with the room as the daughter grows up. A custom linen white "Chrisinelund" trundle daybed from Country Swedish was chosen, and affords room for games and tea parties as well as sleeping. A French raspberry-and-cream-colored Boutis quilt, circa 1860, was draped over the side of the bed to soften the woodwork. White and vanilla accents were added to keep the colors in the room crisp: a French chest of drawers washed in white, a pair of cream-colored transferware vases fashioned into lamps, an oval mirror with carved crossed laurel leaves painted in white and gold leaf hung above a curved-back sofa from O. Henry House, which nestles against the wall.

Eclectic, comfortable and yet timeless and sophisticated, this is a family residence that will be enjoyed for generations to come.

OVERLEAF: The kitchen is a masculine laboratory of stone, copper and brass. The island helps separate the cooking areas and is lit by a trio of hanging copper pendant lights from Oly. The mudroom and family lockers are glimpsed beyond.

Farrow & Ball "Cooking Apple Green" on the ceiling makes the younger daughter's bedroom bright and inviting. Walls are upholstered in a Raoul Textiles printed linen in pink and oyster. Frosty, the family Maltese, enjoys supervising activities from the Victorian pouf ottoman from Hickory Chair, which is upholstered in raspberry pink "Cameo Borscht," the fabric also used for "Emma's Child's Chair" and ottoman from Country Swedish, as well as the soft valenced window draperies, *below*.
■ Pretty and pink is perfect for the teenage daughter's bathroom, which is tiled with Bizazza iridescent glass mosaic tiles. Walls are painted in Benjamin Moore "Fruit Shake," and pink accents include a spool table, ceramic garden seat and Venetian glass vases. The watercolors of butterflies were hand painted and specially commissioned for the room through Evelyn Avery Fine Art,

above right. ▪ Her master bath was designed as an exotic Venetian grotto of sea blue and green mosaic tiles and stonework. Taupe hand-embroidered Christopher Norman taffeta draperies frame French doors opening onto a private terrace that overlooks the gardens and pool, *below right.*

THE UPPER MEZZANINE, DESIGNED FOR FAMILY GATHERINGS,

is furnished with artwork and easily movable furniture. An antique Oushak carpet in muted celadon,
beige and ecru complements the textured walls. The nineteenth-century French gilt chandelier is fitted with strings
of seedpods and bamboo rather than crystals, for a more informal, organic note.

- Don't shortchange the children—give them a beautiful room they can enjoy and they will grow up with an appreciation of good design.

- Hang a collection of framed art tightly together like a windowpane to give it more power and impact.

- Upholster the walls of a noisy room such as a dining room or child's bedroom to absorb sound.

- A large dining room can be made more intimate with smaller settees or tea tables for extra dining.

- Hide a flat-screen TV with shuttered panels of hinged prints or artwork.

ARTS AND CRAFTS IN A WOODLAND GLADE

The vaulted family room is designed with a strong Arts and Crafts aesthetic. Hand-forged "Odette" chandeliers from Ironware International hang from the chestnut ceiling trusses. Furnishings include a versatile cluster of six cube hassocks in jade-colored suede from Edelman Leather and an antique cotton and velvet quilt of flying geese, their V formation repeated in the "Ridgefield Checks" carpet underneath.

WHEN THE CLIENTS OF this home contacted Barry, their request was simple: they wanted a residence in harmony with its setting—a wooded glen they had purchased in eastern Virginia. Barry immediately understood what to do: cut down as few trees as possible, nestle the house amongst the forest and leave room for interiors that were open and comfortable for a family of four.

Enamored of the Arts and Crafts movement, the owners wanted their home to reflect hand craftsmanship and attention to detail. So Barry began by looking outside and using nature for his inspiration—choosing a woodsy palette of clay and stone, warm bark and leafy greens, and the pale, misty skylight glimpsed through the canopy overhead. Ferns, vines and leaves from the forest floor were translated into motifs for the interiors, which were accented with beamed ceiling trusses made of recycled forest lumber.

A soaring twenty-six-foot-high vaulted family room became the center of the home. Capped with a wooden ceiling of arching beams made of reclaimed wormy chestnut, the room was centered on a two-story granite fireplace whose wooden mantel was made from an elm tree that had been growing on the site, anchoring the house both physically and psychologically to its setting. Mushroom-colored walls in a birch bark finish added to the organic atmosphere, as did forest birds perched about the room—a pair of lead eagles on the mantel, cast-iron owl andirons in the fireplace and a series of framed seventeenth-century avian wood engravings lined closely together like totems flanking the mantel.

Vibrant linen draperies in a Robert Kime print were deliberately extended above the arched windows to balance the scale of the room, their rods piercing

A striking limed oak *Gothic staircase leads upstairs*.

An eighteenth-century bronze-and-leather side chair adds to the medieval charm, and a limed oak, Arts and Crafts

"Cerusier" table from David Iatesta complements the woodwork, FACING PAGE.

the wooden brackets supporting the ceiling trusses. Furnishings were centered on a back-to-back George Smith sofa in Rubelli "Husky" red chenille. The warm earth tones were repeated in a trellis-patterned custom rug by Elizabeth Eakins in celadon, jade, stone and oxblood. A comfortable "Riata" lounge chair and ottoman from R. Jones covered in spice-colored "Standen" from Morris & Co., a round, carved oak side table from Rose Tarlow, and accessories including a pair of antique lead table lamps reinforced the Craftsman decor.

The foyer was deliberately kept intimate, beckoning visitors with a warm fire flickering in a rough-hewn granite fireplace. Defining space like a circular rug, a mosaic-banded slate disc was inlaid into the floor. A pair of early-twentieth-century Tiffany bronze chairs whose backs are encircled with twining serpents added a primordial accent. Four walnut armchairs upholstered in Gisbert Rentmeister's tapestry-patterned "Westminster Chen" in a welcoming maize colorway surrounded an ottoman covered in warm caramel leather for comfortable seating.

The adjacent main staircase leading to the second-floor bedrooms was based on William Morris's famous staircase at Red House in England, and was similarly constructed of limed oak with crenellated, pointed newel posts. Limed oak was continued for the staircase wall panels; even the air return vent was hand carved in oak for an honest, handcrafted appeal. Texture was added with a sea grass runner bordered with leather banding on the stairs, a three-panel Art Deco screen covered in shimmering pumpkin orange wooden beads and a simple woven basket filled with the bell-shaped blossoms of cadmium yellow forsythia.

A nineteenth-century French hall tree of antelope horns and driftwood greets visitors at the front door, setting the theme of organic craftsmanship.

Beyond the foyer, the loggia continues to blur the boundaries between inside and out with a wall of arched French doors that open onto the flagstone terrace, pool and surrounding woodlands. Purposefully kept informal to reflect the owners' lifestyle, this room is a fusion of hand craftsmanship and design from cultures around the world. The massive stone fireplace is inset with a hand-carved allegorical panel of the family, much like a William Blake woodcut, while the mantel supports a pair of ancient Burmese funerary jars. Two three-hundred-year-old Chinese root wood chairs look out across the forests, whose leaves were brought back inside as ceramic insets scattered across the flagstone floor. "Aspen" wingback chairs from Schumacher were nestled in front of the fireplace, with Turkish footstools at their sides and a set of four African-inspired walnut chairs from Melrose House encircling a gaming table nearby. A "Japanese Vine" carpet from Timothy Paul Associates anchors the space, while wavy, gilded bronze faux bamboo floor lamps from Dessin Fournir provide light for reading a good book in front of a roaring fire.

At the far end of the entry hall lies the elegant music room, its walls faux painted in golden birch bark, echoing the trees outside. The room is lit by an oversized wrought-iron French chandelier from Amy Perlin, hung low like a sculpture over a button-tufted ottoman placed in the center of the room. A handsome walnut Steinway fills one corner and is silhouetted against a hand-painted eighteenth-century French screen mounted as a mural on the wall behind. Victorian bronze wall sconces were given a more organic and informal note by replacing their crystal prisms with wooden beads and seedpods, reflecting the family's casual lifestyle.

THE INTIMATE FOYER IS CENTERED ON A STONE FIREPLACE

rather than the traditional mirror. Panache "Balboa Iron Sconces" complement the antique
chandelier, *facing*. ▪ A circular inset of mosaic tiles and stone in the foyer
takes the place of a carpet and lends an interplay of textures for an Arts and Crafts appeal, *above*.

The music room is glimpsed through the portal of a gilt convex mirror on the wall. Snowball, the family's West Highland terrier, enjoys the button-tufted ottoman upholstered in Gisbert Rentmeister chenille. Comfortable seating includes a Baker sofa and upholstered Melrose House chairs from Holly Hunt with gilded legs suggesting musical notes, FACING PAGE.

Upstairs the master suite overlooks natural springs and a pool behind the house where warm mists swirling up were used as inspiration. Hazy, underwatery "Hydrangea," another printed linen from Robert Kime, in aqua, celadon, pale salmon, sage and cinnabar, was selected to cover the walls as well as envelop the windows and half-tester bed. A pressed-tin, crenellated border was added to the tops of the window valances and bed for a Gothic note of fairy-tale romance. A plaid wool drugget carpet in placid cream and beige tones from Elizabeth Eakins lies underneath.

The adjoining sitting room is separated from the master bedroom by a double-sided fireplace. It was furnished with well-worn antiques that could have been handed down in the family—a pair of 1920s open-back side chairs with their original faux caning in a Swedish-inspired vanilla and turquoise, a Georgian tea caddy and attentive Staffordshire dogs on the mantel top. A plasma-screen TV waits behind the shirred panels of an old English breakfront.

The master bath is tiled in tumbled Botticino marble mosaics in watery hues of jade, stone and celadon, creating an underwater grotto; an abstracted leaf-and-vine mural painted on the ceiling and upper walls suggests a foggy woodlands. Tapering Arts and Crafts columns (which pop open for storage) separate alcoves for his and her sinks (his is slightly taller) that were created in cast stone and decorated with motifs of the forests, leaves, trailing vines and songbirds.

The morning and breakfast room off the kitchen overlooks the surrounding woodlands and rear terraces. "Dandelion Clock Faded," a colorful printed linen from Robert Kime in duck egg blue, ecru, sage and cranberry, was used for the draperies; these colors are complemented in the blue-green irregular flagstone

On the piano, a rare, c. 1800, black basalt and gilded Wedgwood lumiere from Gore Dean Antiques celebrates music and knowledge.

slabs on the floor. Antique rush-seated French chinoiserie side chairs washed in celadon green with cranberry accents, sage-colored wicker armchairs from Janus et Cie and an antique French settee are pulled up to a Formations "Spanish" gateleg dining table with its base washed in a celery green. Amusing antique accessories keep the room light and enjoyable—a weathered shoe shine stand used for magazines, a rabbit candy mold set under a cloche glass dome on the dining table like a visitor from the forest, a leaded bird sculpture alighted on the table-top.

The woodlands are brought inside the dining room as well, with walls covered in a hand-painted mural of a shady glen overlaid with Morris's "Daisy" pattern. A pendant grape chandelier was customized with bronze castings of actual grape leaves taken from vines on the fence post outside. The theme of grapes and drink were repeated in an antique gilded mirror encircled with a border of entwining grapes placed above the limed oak buffet. The windows are hung with shimmery Fortuny "Orsini" draperies that cascade to the floor and add to the feeling of dining in a thicket of ferns. A dining table in pearwood, olivewood and burled walnut was custom designed through New Classics, with leaves in an organic, lotus shape; the table can enlarge to seat up to sixteen for dinner. "Regence" dining chairs from Niermann Weeks covered in "Butterfly," a Voghi brocade of marigolds, olives and stone grays, add an inviting note of comfort.

Filled with hand-fashioned objects inspired by nature, this home is a true reflection of its sylvan setting. Celebrating with an Arts and Crafts sensibility, it is honest to both its environment and its owners' lifestyle.

The loggia overlooks the rear terraces and woodlands and is a fusion of new and old Arts and Crafts craftsmanship from across the globe. Cooled by an antique-style ceiling fan from The Woolen Mill Co., the room was hand painted in an abstract woodsy finish. Floral-patterned "Sansovino" curtains from Clarence House frame the French doors and help soften the flagstone floor and granite mantel. Note the framed herbieres, which, grouped on the far wall, screen the plasma television behind, *left*. ▪ Leaves blown inside are captured in ceramic insets in the flagstone floors from Milestone Floors, *below*.

Above the master suite, "Hydrangea" is continued on the walls of the loft, furnished with daybeds under the eaves. A carved owl tobacco stand in the center stores pencils and drawing supplies. Generous drawers beneath the daybeds are used for extra storage, *above left*. The master bedroom's cast-stone mantel from Formations and an antique, gilded

wooden mirror resting on top lend a mystical, underwater feeling. Antiques, including a lead finial and French enamelware jug, echo the watery patina, *facing below.* ▪ The sitting room and master bedroom beyond are both upholstered in woodsy Robert Kime "Hydrangea" as a paper-backed linen; the fabric is repeated in the bed hangings and window curtains. A trefoil ottoman from O. Henry House provides extra seating. Bedside lighting includes antique table lamps on the round pedestal table and recessed lighting inside the Lewis Mittman half tester bed, *above.*

The master bath is divided into his and her alcoves by square, tapering columns that contain built-in storage cabinets for toiletries on their sides. The oval mirrors are French antiques. A patchwork of stone squares and rectangles on the floor is continued in the mosaic tilework on the walls. A Kohler Jacuzzi overlooks the rear terraces and woodlands, *above.* ▪ Hand-painted antique metal wall sconces echo the curves of the bedroom's "Hydrangea" wallpaper, *left.* ▪ Cast-stone "Granada" pedestal sinks from Stoneyards are capped with a custom celery gray concrete washbowl. The Anichini terry cloth towel on the right repeats the vine motif. Faucets are "Etoile" from Waterworks, *facing.*

The morning and breakfast room off the kitchen is furnished with comfortable and whimsical antiques. An "Auberge" lounge chair from Formations has removable side wings and is upholstered in Robert Kime "Bird's Nest" printed linen. Curtains are a colorful strawberry and leaf linen from Robert Kime, with "Bentley Ticking Stripe" banding from Brunschwig and Fils. The overhead lantern is French, from Gore Dean Antiques.

THE DINING ROOM CELEBRATES WINE

with an illuminated alabaster grape chandelier and a nineteenth-century gilt bronze stag's head vessel on the table underneath. The buffet was custom designed through Niermann Weeks in limed oak, with a concrete top for a less shiny look. An Elizabeth Eakins "Union Field" rug in shady tones anchors the room.

Barry's Tips

- Bring the woods inside with organic colors and murals of forests.

- A fireplace in the foyer welcomes people inside and makes even a large home intimate and welcoming.

- Extend draperies above the window to make the window seem taller.

- Antiques are environmentally conscious, green decorating—no new trees are cut down.

- Incorporate nature's basic elements of earth, air, fire and water for a naturally balanced interior.

EMBASSY ELEGANCE IN WASHINGTON, D.C.

The original staircase gracefully curves up from the foyer and sets the tone for the rest of the home. Wooden drops instead of crystals make the iron-and-gilt "Palazzo" chandelier from Dennis & Leen less formal. An antique Bechstein piano rests in the front bay. Draperies are Bergamo's "Prisca" cream silk.

WASHINGTON IS A CITY known for its broad boulevards lined with elegant townhomes, many of them former private mansions now put to official use. One such building, an imposing Beaux Arts mansion, was built in the late nineteenth century for a wealthy heiress. Converted into an embassy in the early twentieth century, it had been divided into a warren of tiny offices by the time the current owners purchased it in 2003; fortunately, its structure and detailing were still largely intact. The grand, sweeping staircase with ornate bronze railings had never been altered, handsome trim work and wall paneling remained untouched, and the ornate plasterwork ceilings had been preserved beneath dropped acoustic tile ceilings. Barry worked closely with the owners and their architects to return the building to its original grandeur as a single-family residence, a process that took more than two years.

Five stories tall, the residence was built as a townhouse, with deep, vertical rooms. As the new owners wished to use the home frequently for entertaining, a new kitchen, wine cellars and bathrooms were added on the lower level. The first floor continued as the entrance and main level of the house, the enfilade of rooms unified with natural, warm colors—washed whites and taupe hand painted with a striated finish on the original paneled walls. To emphasize the home's timelessness, Botticino and Noce marble floors were installed in twenty-four-inch diagonal blocks and given a vinegar wash for a muted shine; borders of tumbled mosaic tiles frame the field for a finished look. The commanding, open staircase, which sweeps up four stories, was carefully conserved; its gilded bronze railings were left intact but updated with an upper rail for modern code requirements. Classic furnishings were selected—a pair

A HAND-PAINTED ITALIAN CHAIR

from Niermann Weeks is upholstered with gold silk damask from Schumacher, its pattern and
color a pleasing contrast against the crusty mosaic tile floor, *above.* ▪
Deep and narrow, the townhome greets guests in an elegant enfilade of rooms from front entry
to dining room, each separated by a broad archway. The classic foyer, with
hand-painted paneled walls in striated cream and limestone finish by Warnock Studios and
complementary marble-tiled floors, is furnished with a "Baroque" console from Dennis
& Leen, Baker wingback chairs and an open-backed "Roseanne" side chair from Tomlinson near
the staircase. Rich and warm fabrics include a gold Rubelli silk brocade pillow, *facing.*

THE LIVING ROOM IS CENTERED ON A HANDSOME REGENCY PARLOR

table from Randall Tysinger. A new hand-carved mantel and a detailed plasterwork ceiling whose cornices were recast
and applied from fragments of the original through Ornamental Plasterworks add architectural
interest. A pair of gilded "Belle Fleur" mirrors in rectangular panes from Panache rest above Amy Howard's "Wave Consoles"
on either side of the mantel, *above*. ▪ An "Osray" lantern from Christopher Norman echoes
the plaster ceiling's roundels and latticework grid added during restoration. The cornice molding is original, *right*.

of early Irish wing chairs from Baker upholstered in "Imperatore," a figured chenille from Quadrille; stone pedestals carved with swags and garlands supporting antique Italian lidded marble urns; an oval eighteenth-century gilded French mirror. A vintage Bechstein piano was imported from Germany to rest in the front bay, and an upholstered settee from Panache nestled against the staircase, the perfect spot to sit back and enjoy the music.

The living room opens directly off the foyer through a gracefully arched, cased doorway. A formal drawing room meant for entertaining, its paneled walls were painted with creamy Benjamin Moore "Greenmount Silk" and detailing was highlighted with Farrow & Ball "New White"—colors that glow at night when the lights are low and a fire is lit in the fireplace. (Barry recommends warm colors for conversation, avoiding pale blues and grays). Silk draperies in Bergamo "Tornabuoni" in maize, gold and coppery orange complement the cream and celery-green tones of the antique Oushak carpet underneath; their traditional swags and panels were deliberately lightened with simple iron curtain rods for a more streamlined and modern appeal.

A Regency rosewood center table welcomes guests, and comfortable seating is loosely clustered about the room—light, wheel-backed side chairs from Lewis Mittman, a comfortable Rose Tarlow "Verona" armchair, and near the bay window Tarlow's classic lyre-shaped "Faringale" wing chairs covered in a warm terra-cotta "Chinois" silk from Christopher Norman.

Fine antiques add focal points of interest—a pair of Empire bronze-and-gold candlesticks converted to lamps rest on a gilded and carved "Wave Console" from Amy Howard; nineteenth-century Minton transferware plates hang in a column on the wall; a gilt bronze-and-jade French epergne

corner of the living room shows the sophisticated and muted palette of Benjamin Moore "Greenmount Silk" walls highlighted with Farrow & Ball "Farrow's Cream" and "New White" accents. Traditional drapery swags, adorned with trim from Watts of Westminster, are modernized with simple wrought-iron curtain rods. The front bay window provides views of the bustling capital and is centered with a nineteenth-century English gilded walnut library table. ▪ The warm, masculine library is upholstered in citron yellow and orange "Cornwall" from Bergamo. A handsome plaster ceiling adds more intimacy. A pair of R. Jones maize velvet "Lassiter" chairs flanks the Knoll sofa from George Smith. A Fortuny "Scudo Sarceno" pendant lamp hangs overhead, *facing*.

Another view of the comfortably furnished library. *A Baker Regency-style* card table rests in front of the window. Note the subtle repetition of patterns: angles of the sea grass rug are echoed in the plaster ceiling's roundels, while wooden fringe on the soft pelmet pulls in the adjacent dining room's woodwork, FACING PAGE.

on the center table reflects the pale green and gold accents used throughout the room.

The adjacent library was opened into the living room with folding pocket doors to enhance circulation and transform the rooms into one large reception space when needed. A warm palette of saffron and yolky golds was created with Bergamo "Cornwall" lampas used as upholstery on the walls and continued as the curtain pelmet and panels for the broad central window. An ornate plaster ceiling was added for more interest, highlighted by a Fortuny hand-painted silk pendant chandelier. Exotic furnishings were chosen to reference the room's original function as an embassy—a leather-and-bronze ottoman from Istanbul, a Persian floor lamp from Jamie Young—and mixed with classic seating, including a "Tiplady" Knoll sofa from George Smith covered in Bergamo "Byron" gold ribbed velvet, a pair of "Swift" lounge chairs from Beaumont & Fletcher upholstered in orange woven silk ("Allure" from Bergamo), and next to the sofa two smaller pull-up "Lassiter" chairs from R. Jones covered in Quadrille "Georgia," a maize cut velvet. The library was given a masculine note by incorporating large brass studs throughout the room—to outline the upholstered wall panels, anchor the perimeter of the leather ottoman, accent the lounge chairs, and even finish the border of the sea grass carpet underneath.

A handsome pearwood-and-burled-walnut dining table from New Classics was custom designed for the dining room, its expandable lotus-shaped leaves able to seat up to forty-two for dinner. Exquisite seventeenth-century oak floral carvings by the famous English Restoration carver Grinling Gibbons flank the mantel; original to the room, they were uncovered during remodeling and carefully conserved. Woodwork throughout was skillfully brought back to life: walnut paneling on the walls blackened with age was refinished and lightened to highlight its beautiful grain.

A plaster ceiling of Gothic quatrefoils contained in a grid was added overhead, the design subtly repeated in a scalloped, chenille border from Gisbert Rentmeister banded onto the

sea grass carpet. Bronze cherubs firmly hold early-nineteenth-century marble-and-gilt dore candelabras on the table, while a pair of Victorian zinc horse heads with original gilt finish surveys the diners from the wall behind. French doors across the back leading to the rear terrace were hung with simple Conrad woven "Bark of Sari Trees" shades for privacy but still allow filtered sunlight to stream into the room. Dining chairs from R. Jones were covered in a golden floral silk lampas from Hass, button tufted on their seats and down their backs for an elegant, more modern and tailored look.

Upstairs bedroom suites were created for the owners, their children and overnight guests. The guest suite attends to every need of its occupants with a "Circolo" console writing desk from Niermann Weeks for writing letters or working on the computer, custom-designed, mirrored armoires for clothing (and to conceal a television), and even a comfortable chair and ottoman from O. Henry House for curling up in front of the fireplace on a chilly winter evening. The Federal-style "Verada," Wilton rug pattern of decorative rosettes and circles set within squares from Stark was repeated in a plaster ceiling of rondels inset in a latticework grid. A Julia Gray Regency four-poster bed and canopy anchor the room; the bed is dressed with warm Hodsoll McKenzie florals—raspberry-and-cream "Wild Bramble" on the coverlet and "Elvedon" on the box-pleated canopy.

Created from a spare room, the master bath is a private retreat unto itself. With its own stone fireplace, it's a luxurious room, a place to relax with a cup of tea at the circa 1870 Italian mosaic side table and chairs sensibly covered in terry cloth Anichini towels. A freestanding claw-foot tub finished with matte nickel fittings is perfect for long, relaxing soaks, while a glass-enclosed steam shower is available nearby. A pair of "Iron Etching" Kohler sinks was set into an onyx-topped console that is supported by iron legs custom forged to Barry's design. Across the room, an overscaled freestanding Oly cabinet holds towels and toiletries. The floors are tiled in the same Botticino and Noce marble as in the foyer but in a different octagon and dot pattern that is carried eigh-

teen inches up the walls to provide extra protection from errant splashes and to break the room's verticality. French doors opening to a private balcony are covered with draperies in Scalamandré "Salome" printed linen in putty, chocolate and citron to help absorb sound and add another note of luxury.

Scalamandré "Salome" was continued in the adjoining master bedroom for the window draperies and bed hangings to liaison with the master bath. Centered on a classic four-poster "Prince Charles" canopied bed from Rose Tarlow, the room is designed for comfort and repose. A two-seat "Alexandra" sofa from Beaumont and Fletcher in a soothing "Ricepaper" mohair velvet is an inviting spot to spend a quiet moment reading the morning paper, while Amy Howard's gessoed "Custom Wave" table in the bay window is just right for a leisurely breakfast or tea for two. The grid of the bathroom's marble floor is repeated in a softer material—a maize-colored cut-wool carpet from Stark ("Illyse"), and the circle-and-grid pattern is reflected as well on the custom plaster ceiling. Soft textiles in soothing taupes, mochas and creams add to the feeling of calm throughout the room: the bed is draped in Scalamandré linen with inner linings of taupe Schumacher "Shenandoah Check," while comfortable "Tub" chairs from Beaumont and Fletcher are upholstered in a creamy, figured chenille from J. Lambeth & Co.

A family room and kitchen were created from several unused bedrooms across from the master suite for convenience and to diminish the need for traveling between floors. Kept open for easy circulation, a center cooking island and breakfast bar in the kitchen is highlighted by four angular floor-to-ceiling quarter-sawn oak columns, anchoring the area without blocking light or visual access. The adjoining family room is warm, open and decidedly more modern, decorated with African and ethnic art reflecting the family's travels. Walls are covered in Donghia natural raffia, and windows are draped with Boussac's botanical French linen print "Ombre" hung from bamboo rings and rods for a hint of the tropics. An olive-and-tan, handwoven wool carpet from Odegard anchors a sofa and loveseat from O. Henry House covered in Donghia goldenrod "Krazy Quilt Matelasse," while a Panache "Barcelona" walnut gaming table across the room provides an area for taking light meals as well as playing games. Zulu jugs, a silver-metallic-embroidered Tunisian textile framed over the mantel and an African stool from Botswana add to the South African ambience.

Sympathetically and intelligently conserved and restored, this former embassy has been rescued from institutional life and returned to its original design—as an elegant and classic cosmopolitan home.

Walnut paneling and a quatre-foil plasterwork ceiling give the dining room the feel of an old English club. Wood carvings above the mantel were discovered during renovation and identified as the work of Grinling Gibbons, the famed seventeenth-century English woodcarver, *above*. ▪ Dining chairs are tailor fitted with Haas's silk brocade "Aristeo," which is complemented by the curving "Westminster" chenille banding from Gisbert Rentmeister on the sea grass carpet. *above right*. ▪ A nineteenth-century zinc horse head with gilt detailing from Gore Dean Antiques is one of a pair that adds a lighter note to the formal setting, *right*.

A family kitchen on the second floor is designed for convenience. Columns of limed, waxed oak have touch-latched, recessed cabinets for extra storage and to separate the cooking and food preparation area. Light pours through an art glass cabinet above the sink. A lava-stone Kohler sink and custom acid-washed copper hood by Ron Kelly add an industrial note. A screen of framed engravings commissioned through Avery Fine Art obscures a TV screen, *above.* ▪ Blenko glass amber and green jars rest on a side table in the family room, their hues reflected in the botanical-print draperies from Boussac. The lamp is made from a vintage zinc architectural fragment found in Paris, while the table is Barry's own design for Tomlinson, *left.* ▪ A walnut gaming table from Panache also functions for meals and is lit by a pendant "Madeline" fixture from Paul Ferrante. The chairs from Randall Tysinger Antiques are antique English Jacobean style with their original leather upholstery intact. Charleston Forge bar stools at the breakfast bar are upholstered in Henry Calvin "High Life" linen. A glowing orange Chihuly glass sculpture rests on the mantel, *facing.*

The Prince Charles four-poster bed from Rose Tarlow is classically inspired with subtly lacquered vines winding up the posts. Accent pillows include "Orsini," a Fortuny celery and silvery gold silk. A "Feather" side chair from Melrose House is pulled up to a "Baroda" writing desk from Formations, *above*. ▪ Befitting its location in the nation's capital, the guest suite is anchored with Stark's Federal-style Wilton "Verada" carpet in soft cocoa and brown, whose colors are complemented by Farrow & Ball "Farrow's Cream" walls. Classic furnishings include a Julia Gray four-poster canopy bed, a button-tufted chair and ottoman in Coraggio textured velvet in front of the fireplace and an antique, bronze lantern overhead, *facing*.

THE MASTER BATH exudes subtle luxury—a cozy fireplace, handsome marble tiles carried up the walls, even a table for tea in front of the fire. The frosted glass armoire from Oly is used for storage. Bronze "Beverly" wall sconces from 20th Century Lighting above the mantel add a soft glow. The garden seat is Vietnamese, *facing*. ▪ A pair of Lewis Mittman chairs upholstered in ivory terry cloth Anichini towels flanks the antique marble-topped table in front of the fireplace, *left*. ▪ Views of the nation's capital are enjoyed from the bay window in the master bedroom. Window and bed curtains of Scalamandré silk "Salome" tie the bedroom to the master bath. Tub chairs from Beaumont and Fletcher in England are upholstered in "Portico" chenille and rest around the "Custom Wave" table from Amy Howard, *below*.

Barry's Tips

- Use warm, stimulating colors for conversation areas—fireglow reds, ember oranges and golds.

- Don't be afraid of decorative plaster ceilings. They add architectural interest and can subtly reinforce patterns in the room's furnishings.

- The perfect host anticipates all of a guest's needs and includes areas for correspondence, TV and relaxing in the guest room.

- A bathroom can be more than functional—include an area to relax, a table for tea or a fireplace.

- Travel mementoes—especially handcrafted and ethnic pieces—make striking accents and mix well with modern design.

SUMMER MEMORIES ON THE DELAWARE SHORE

The ground-floor entry collects souvenirs of the beach: painted tin sunflowers set in a garden bin for weeds, a nineteenth-century mailbox from a seaside hotel in France, a grape harvest basket filled with beach balls.

AFTER PURCHASING AN oceanfront lot on the sunny eastern Delaware shore, these clients contacted Barry and explained what they wanted: an informal summer retreat that could withstand not only the water and sand but also four active children and their friends, two Hungarian Vizslas and frequent guests. Something summery and easy to live with but still formal enough to entertain. A home that would be special enough to provide long-lasting memories of enjoyable family summers at the shore.

Working with architect John Olivieri, Barry began designing from the inside out. Special waterfront considerations had to be addressed: the ground floor needed to be waterproof and resilient to winter storms; thus, lava-stone flooring was installed throughout the lower entertainment level. The primary shared living spaces were placed above, along with au pair's quarters. An open, tightly spiraling staircase was designed leading to bedroom suites on the third floor—children's and guest rooms, as well as a commons area for games and projects on the mezzanine. An adult sanctuary was created on the fourth floor, with a master suite and private decks overlooking the ocean, and across the hall a cozy crow's nest for family guests, tucked into the octagonal turret.

The entry sets the tone for the home. Centered on a tumbled-marble mosaic compass inlaid in the floor, the foyer points visitors in all directions: to the left the living and dining rooms, straight ahead the kitchen and service areas, and to the right the staircase connecting to the other floors. A grand eighteenth-century Gustavian table with octopus-like legs holds center court and is complemented by watercolors hung on the concave wall behind—flowers commissioned from John Matthew Moore that reflect the colors of the house: vermillion red, fern green, sunset orange and yellow. All the seriousness is

Each of the children has *his or her own drawer for ice cream money* and special keepsakes in the old cabinet; the child's rush-seated chair still has its original red paint. An antique French advertising sign hangs above, FACING PAGE.

relieved with a 1950s toile painted lamp turned into an amusing candelabra, reminding us that this is still just a beach house. The staircase spirals upward with unique risers inspired by the end of a clothespin, a design chosen to allow more light to filter through the tightly turning steps. Crafted in bleached cherry, the steps and railings were painted in "Lime White" from Benjamin Moore for a clean, summery look. The staircase is a piece of sculpture to greet visitors, functioning as the vertebrae of the house, yet still usable and sturdy enough for daily use.

Ocean views were the objective for the living room design, so a soaring, light-filled space was created with an expansive bank of glazed windows stretching across the entire back wall. Light streams into the room as the sun rises over the ocean each morning inspiring the helios palette of luminous yellows, sunrise oranges and reds and sparkling golds.

Centered on an overscaled, two-story fireplace with a cast-stone mantel, the living room was furnished with items chosen to reflect Greco-Roman classicism but still with a focus on the sea: a pair of nineteenth-century shell-encrusted French urns on the mantel, a salvaged terra-cotta capital perhaps dredged from the ocean depths now converted into a side table, a pair of netlike wheel-backed side chairs. Walls were given a dappled finish in the colors of the sand dunes outside. An antique desk once owned by Sister Parish and marbleized by her in

The seriousness of an eighteenth-century gilded, Gustavian table in the entry is relieved by a 1950s lamp turned candelabra.

the deep garnet tones of a glowing fire was placed at the front of the room, with a French glazed terra-cotta sphinx resting on top—a siren calling sailors to an enchanted place beneath the waves. Sunny Bergamo printed linen draperies in a narrow yellow-and-white stripe help anchor the large room, framing the views while softening the bright light from the sea.

A hand-carved wooden lattice screen of abstract crosses and circles, inspired by ancient Hellenistic engravings, partitions the adjacent dining room while allowing diners to enjoy the living room vistas. Geometric allegories define this space, whose curved walls are echoed by the round sea grass carpet and circular walnut dining table. The ceiling was lowered to eight feet to make the room more intimate, and classical accents were added, including a pair of eighteenth-century leaded Italian urns on chiseled African stone pedestals nestled into the curved bank of windows overlooking the ocean. Colors were kept bright and sunny, the dining chairs upholstered in mustard-and-blood-orange-striped linen from Creation Baumann, while the waves of the ocean were brought inside via a salvaged nineteenth-century chandelier with verdigris undulating arms floating overhead.

Elegant and classic but still informal, the dining room opens into the breakfast bar and kitchen. Inspired by the light-filled ambience of the south of France, birch cabinets were finished with a mellow, Dijon yellow wash and implements of beach life were hung overhead—wicker baskets

SUNSHINE FILLS the two-story living room overlooking the ocean. A glaze terra-cotta Sphinx sits on a desk that once belonged to Sister Parish and is flanked by antique mercury glass candlestick lamps from David Bell Antiques. The comfortable Tomlinson sofa is upholstered in a sunshine yellow textured chenille from Rubelli, while a Regency-style Schumacher chaise is a favorite spot for relaxing and watching the fire and sea.

Pelicans are a popular theme at the shore, and a flock has lit on an antique terra-cotta capital (from Gore Dean Antiques) made into an end table with a modern concrete top, FACING PAGE.

for impromptu picnics, copper pots and pans and old tin pails from Vermont for collecting clams. A five-shelved antique Irish pine plate rack on the end of one counter was stacked with yellow ware plates and dishes from France, an echo of the morning sunrise. Adjacent to the kitchen, the casual breakfast room looks out over the ocean. Practicality was the key—a trestle table and benches for the inevitable wet swim suits and sand were chosen. Benches were enlivened with corncob graining in ketchup red and Dijon yellow. Cabana-striped canvas shades from Osborne and Little in cheerful citrus colors added a festive note. At the end of the room a crusty early-nineteenth-century painted French armoire with a translucent wire mesh door was filled with colorful enamelware for easy dining.

A children's commons was created on the third-floor mezzanine, an open area shielded from stair hall traffic by a tall back settle upholstered in an Osborne and Little fabric. The perfect spot for summer craft projects or just watching TV, the commons also doubles as an extra spot for young overnight guests.

Across the hall, the daughter's room is upholstered with a Manuel Canovas fabric of fuchsia pink and sunshine yellow, cheerful colors that spark fond memories of the beach during the dark winter months. Furnished with two trundle daybeds from Country Swedish and a dreamy hammock in the corner, the room is comfortable for sleepovers. The fanciful wrought-iron flowers from a mid-century console used as an occasional table between the windows were continued into the bath, where they were recycled as a delicate decorative screen over the mirror.

Golds, ambers and yellows—
the colors of the sun rising over the ocean—radiate from the antique Waterford crystal globe that rests on a "Nettie Darr" steel mesh table from Mike Reid Weeks in the center of the living room.

Ships and the sea were the themes for the young boys' room. Two sets of bunk beds with pullout trundles sleep up to six youngsters, with enough space for desks at the end of each bunk. Country Swedish wallpaper lets the boys wake up under a starry, sunset orange sky. Nautical accessories, including old wooden buoys and a crusty anchor discovered in an Eastern Shore shop, help make the room shipshape and seaworthy for adventurous and energetic boys.

The fourth floor and top level of the home serves as a retreat for the adults. A generous master suite is entered through a romantic, turreted antechamber highlighted with cast-plaster ribs anchoring the vaulted ceiling. Tangerine-and-lemon printed draperies from Sacho Hesslein block out the early morning sun but still lend a warm, golden glow. Across the central foyer, a cozy guest suite is tucked into another turret. A circular captain's table is a cozy spot for gazing out over the ocean and can be kept private for late-night reading by panels from Old World Weavers that are scrimmed from the ceiling. The headboard is ruched in the same golden toile. Walls are painted in "Yellow Maize" from Benjamin Moore, yellows and golds playing against each other throughout the room. More curved trusses set into the ceiling above the bed cleverly disguise the room's angularity and subtly soften it to the unsuspecting eye.

Now more than a decade old, this beach house remains one of the clients' favorite summer escapes, a magical place to relax and enjoy the beauty of the shore in a home filled with laughter, happy memories and abundant sunshine.

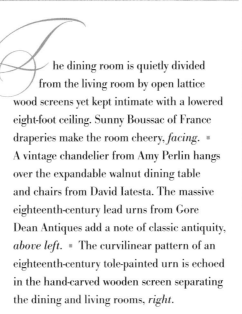

*T*he dining room is quietly divided from the living room by open lattice wood screens yet kept intimate with a lowered eight-foot ceiling. Sunny Boussac of France draperies make the room cheery, *facing*. ▪ A vintage chandelier from Amy Perlin hangs over the expandable walnut dining table and chairs from David Iatesta. The massive eighteenth-century lead urns from Gore Dean Antiques add a note of classic antiquity, *above left*. ▪ The curvilinear pattern of an eighteenth-century tole-painted urn is echoed in the hand-carved wooden screen separating the dining and living rooms, *right*.

A breakfast bar separates the kitchen from the dining room; the potting room and laundry is glimpsed beyond. Custom cabinets from Premier Cabinetry were accented with bead board for a casual country appeal. The bar stools from Charleston Forge are covered in vinyl-coated linen to prevent stains from wet bathing suits, *facing.* ▪ Morning sun streams into the kitchen; the colors are repeated in the yellow plates stacked in an antique pine plate rack from Gore Dean Antiques. Rosy orange marble countertops and a mustard wash over the lower cabinets add to the room's glow. The slag glass pendant light is from Rejuvenation, *above left.* ▪ The breakfast room, just steps away from the beach, is casual and convenient. A trestle table (Guy Chaddock) and vintage benches, an antique painted armoire (Amy Perlin) for dishes and bowls, and a tole-painted antique iron chandelier add to the appeal, *below left.*

A CLOTHESPIN was Barry's inspiration for the eye-catching design of the stairs, which spiral to the upper floors, *left*. ▪ The five rooms of the master suite are entered through the vaulted antechamber; the main bedchamber is to the left. An antique walnut table from Gore Dean Antiques is handy for an early morning coffee while watching the sun rise over the ocean. Bare hardwood floors reflect the light. Blanket chest from Rose Tarlow; mirrored wall sconces from Vaughn, *facing*.

THE BOYS' ROOM CAN SLEEP UP TO SIX YOUNGSTERS

with a pair of trundle bunk beds. Seaside antiques found in local shops and Country Swedish wallpaper
adds to the charm, *above*. ▪ Bold colors work well in summer homes as they are used for only part of the year.
Here the teenage daughter's room is swathed in hot pink and sunny yellow fabrics from Manuel Canovas.
Trundle daybeds and whitewashed tea table from Country Swedish. Pendant lamp from Vaughn, *facing*.

Barry's Tips

- Keep the sun shining all year round by using textiles inspired by its light—tangerine, lemon yellow, orange, red and gold.

- Disguise the angularity of a ceiling with arched trusses and coved moldings.

- Don't be afraid to downplay a serious antique with an amusing accent to keep it from becoming too formal and unapproachable.

- A lowered ceiling instantly makes a dining room more intimate.

- The foyer gives a hint of what is to come—subtly suggest colors and elements around the corner to entice visitors inside.

The fourth-floor guest suite is tucked into a turret, its walls painted a sunny yellow. The ruched headboard and curtains are an Old World Weavers toile. Raffia shades top a pair of simple floor lamps (Jamie Young) and an antique sailing ship diorama above, from Miller & Arny Antiques, continues the theme of the sea, *facing far left*. ▪ A spot for ship building or gazing out over the ocean can be kept private with scrimmed curtains from Old World Weavers, *facing*. ▪ A commons room for the children's crafts, games and slumber parties is the focal point of the third-floor mezzanine. An Osborne and Little animal cotton print covers the settle and hangs as portieres, *above*.

COTSWOLDS CHARM IN VIRGINIA

The living room functions as a study and music room as well. An English Victorian oil of a pastoral scene hangs above the quartersawn oak fireplace. Four comfortable Kindle club chairs are covered in espresso-colored "D'Braun" chenille from Gisbert Rentmeister and accented with Edwardian-style flowers hand appliquéd in metallic threads. One of a set of six nineteenth-century side chairs, with its original, gold metallic embroidery still intact, rests next to the fireplace. A cocoa-colored sea grass carpet anchors the room.

THE COTSWOLDS IS ONE of the loveliest areas of England. Narrow, hedge-lined lanes wind through picturesque villages of small thatched cottages, making it sometimes hard to believe you are in the twenty-first century. Such idyllic countryside is what inspired this 5,000-square-foot home in eastern Virginia. The owners made several trips to England just to acquaint themselves with the region, photographing and taking notes of the soft gray stone houses and details they especially liked. Armed with their wish lists, they contacted architect Russell Versaci to design a home and asked Barry to create its interiors. For over a year, they all met at the site each week to review details and designs before construction even began. The homeowners enjoy entertaining and are warm and hospitable by nature, thus the main goal was to reflect their personalities with a friendly, welcoming home, a Cotswolds cottage refined for an American lifestyle.

The tone was set in the entry hall, which is warm and welcoming with the character of a Wallace Nutting print. A community table is nestled in the corner against a curvaceous banquette—just the spot to set a glass of wine while taking off your coat. In fact, a vineyard is introduced with Bergamo's "Cana Rubin," a claret-colored weave of grapes and vines used to upholster the banquette's seat and back. Informality is accented with a Beaumanier limestone floor, and woodwork throughout is finished in mellow, plain oak, in a nod to the Arts and Crafts aesthetic, specifically William Morris's famous Red House, whose staircase's Gothic newel posts inspired a more modern interpretation here. The textured stucco walls are glazed in tones of warm parchment and toast—an inviting combination.

THE ENTRY LOOKS
inviting with a nook created
from a built-in corner banquette inspired by period
Wallace Nutting illustrations. A
cobbled and chiseled limestone
floor adds to the storybook
appeal. The English walnut tilt-
top table is antique. A French
lantern overhead lends a gentle
glow. The corridor beyond
stretches past the kitchen to
the master bedroom, *left*.
• The plaited sea grass runner
on the stairs is bordered with
chocolate Edelman leather in
a pattern of branches and held
in place with D'Kei antiqued
brass nail heads, *below*.

Floor-to-ceiling oak bookcases run the length of the room to make an accessible, much-used study. The George III table desk is a favorite spot to read. The tufted Beacon Hill ottoman is upholstered in tweedy brown Gisbert Rentmeister "Edison" wool and doubles as a table, FACING PAGE.

Rather than a formal living room, a barrel-vaulted gathering room was added off the entry across the west end of the home. A combination parlor, study and music room, it has the atmosphere of an English men's club, with a classically pillared, quartersawn oak fireplace designed by Versaci and walls paneled in grids of oak to a height of twelve feet. A mahogany "Acanthus" center table from New Classics was surrounded with four Edwardian-style saddle-arm club chairs from Kindle, creating an inviting spot for conversation or a winter dinner in front of the fire. The windows were draped with long panels of Quadrille "Mazarim" woven velvet that are bordered with "Lido" chenille from Gisbert Rentmeister to absorb sound and lend an architectural presence to the soaring walls.

A walnut Steinway baby grand piano in front of the large window is used for musical soirees, while built-in floor-to-ceiling waxed oak bookcases run the length of the room, creating an inviting setting for an open library and study. A George III desk along one side is set with an eighteenth-century Portuguese globe and a pair of gilded candlestick lamps, a quiet spot to read the leather-bound editions of the classics—from Dickens to Poe—lining the shelves.

Beyond the entry, French doors open to the intimate dining room. A coffered ceiling, limestone floors beneath a custom Elizabeth Eakins "Arts and Leaves" wool carpet and a cast-stone fireplace lend a medieval old-world appeal. Softly pleated drapery panels of Quadrille's printed linen "Le Notre Toile" were banded with an edging of yolky yellow quilted

A comfortable "Angles" sofa from Baker nestles in a corner of the living room. A velvet throw pillow with Edwardian metallic embroidery and fringe accents the velvet "Mazarin" draperies from Quadrille.

cotton from Manuel Canovas to frame both the pattern and the view. The drapery's floral motif was abstractly repeated in a wall mural around the room, hand painted by Warnock Studios. "Twist" dining chairs from Guy Chaddock were covered in a textured yellow-and-gold chenille from Watts of Westminster, whose warm tones were repeated in a hand-painted mustard-yellow "Mantuan" tole chandelier from Niermann Weeks. Rather than conventional china cabinets, niches were added on either side of the French doors for greater visual depth. Marble shelves for serving and display were set on top of antique wrought-iron garden gates whose soft curves were subtly repeated in the draperies and wall mural behind.

The large family kitchen beyond the dining room was divided into three main task areas by kitchen designer Mick Di Gulio: cooking and food preparation near the sink and Viking stove; a two-tiered center island and eating bar; and on the opposite side of the room, refrigeration and storage. To enhance the feeling of a thatched and timbered English cottage, reclaimed oak flooring and weathered ceiling beams from a midwestern barn were used. The oak center island and breakfast bar were finished with forest green Vermont soapstone counters and set with comfortable tractor seat–style bar stools from the Wright Table Company.

Additional dining space at the far end of the room was provided by a nineteenth-century farmhouse trestle table and rush-seated ladder-back chairs. A simple iron chandelier from Bruce Eicher hangs overhead, while draperies in Pierre

A large stone fireplace from Renaissance anchors the dining room, giving it the air of a medieval castle. A double-pedestal dining table in burl walnut and olive ash from New Classics can seat up to twelve and is set with an organic wooden tureen filled with flowers to bring in the theme of nature popular in Arts and Crafts interiors, FACING PAGE.

Frey cotton enhance the look of the English countryside with embroidered thistles and banding of warm Stroheim and Romann "Riley Plaid" (repeated in Roman shades over the kitchen sink). A private area for the lady of the house—a keeping room overlooking the herb garden—was set in an alcove in the main hall just outside the kitchen. The inviting nook was furnished with an antique pine French daybed with a Greek fisherman-style mattress upholstered in Pierre Frey "Bellay" cotton ticking, and an apple-picking ladder from Vermont for hanging newspapers and magazines.

For entering the family room off the kitchen, Barry designed large Gothic iron screens. The room was designed by Versaci with a vaulted, antique-timbered ceiling of intersecting trusses and purlins and was centered on a massive granite fireplace at the far end. A pair of rustic wrought-iron chandeliers designed by Barry for Mike Reid Weeks light the room overhead. A William and Mary wing chair from Lee Jofa, a Tomlinson sofa in soft brown chenille, and a pair of bergeres and an ottoman from Rose Tarlow upholstered in a mustard-yellow-and-red-striped woven cotton provided comfortable seating for watching television (which is kept out of view when not in use by a Jacobean-style walnut and pearwood armoire from New Classics). Woodsy floral-printed burlap draperies from Old World Weavers added color and warmth to the banks of windows flanking both sides of the room.

A small glazed garden room behind the family room was held to a modest scale, in keeping with an English sensibility.

Niches on either side of the dining room French doors take the place of china cabinets; garden gates are recycled into handsome grilles with the addition of a marble serving shelf above. Note how the wall murals are a watery, dreamy interpretation of the linen curtains from Quadrille.

African slate tile floors helped bring nature indoors as does a striking century-old South African yew wood table set with a period Arts and Crafts oak chair. Other furnishings—including a woven hyacinth teakwood lounge chair and ottoman—continued the nature theme.

The master suite is reached by way of a light-filled passageway overlooking the gardens and pool. The bedroom's generous fifteen-foot ceiling is finished with a mansard roof outlined with old wooden beams for a note of the French countryside, further enhanced with Old World Weaver's romantic French toile "Voyage En Chine" used to upholster the walls as well as for the curtains and bed hangings. Sanderson's Morris "Willow" lace panels on the windows help filter the sunlight while throwing a delicate, willowy pattern across the plaid, wool carpet. The wooden canopy of a custom cherry "Cupola" bed from New Classics echoes the beams overhead and the relaxing, coffee and cocoa tones of the toile bed hangings are complemented by interior bed curtains of Pierre Frey's lively brown-and-cream-checked linen "Grimaud." Necessities are cleverly camouflaged—an antique porcupine quill box hides the television remote controls at the side of the bed and necessary but unsightly air vents were blended into the upholstered walls by patiently covering each vent with fabric. A favorite spot for relaxing on Saturday mornings is around the fireplace, and comfortable seating is set with a pair of "Victoria" lounge chairs from Rose Tarlow and a Milling Road sofa piled high with cushions at the foot of the bed.

continued on page 126

The kitchen seems straight out of England, with weathered barn beams overhead, recycled floor planks and stuccoed plaster walls. The stone is ornamented with a cast-stone hood and Pratt and Larson tiles of fruits and vegetables on the backsplash, *above*.

The far corner of the kitchen is set for casual dining with an antique oak trestle table. The wheeled wrought-iron console was designed by Barry for Mike Reid Weeks. Hand-colored eighteenth-century botanical drawings subtly echo the earthen tones of the room, *facing*.

*C*eiling beams reclaimed from a mid-western barn add architectural character and also help save trees, *left.* ▪ Salvaged barn ceiling beams are continued into the

The upstairs guest bedroom—an ode to William Morris —had its walls upholstered in his 1890 pattern "Pink and Rose" from Sanderson; the same pattern was also used for the bed coverings and window curtains. A faux bamboo four-poster bed from Julia Gray was placed to face the stone fireplace, and a comfortable lounge nearby was upholstered in a quilted cotton from Bergamo in a pleasing robin's-egg blue. Antique accessories including a carved wooden squirrel lamp and silent-but-wise-owl humidor reflected the countryside theme. The guest bath continued the woodlands motif with walls papered in Morris's "Acorn"; the acorns were repeated in Pratt and Larson tiles behind the bathtub and in the shower. The geometry of the tile's grid work was reinforced with a hand-cut octagonal African slate floor.

A powder room was nestled downstairs off the entry foyer, its cast-stone sink inspired by a baptismal font. An antique gilded Empire mirror over the sink, organic four-inch squares of African slate tile on the walls, and a twisted Chinese root-wood plant stand complete the look of a magical hidden cavern.

Comfortable and inviting, with the charm of the Cotswolds but tailored to an American lifestyle, this home remains a perfect fit for this hospitable family and, as they warmly attest, feels just right.

adjoining family room, which is centered on a two-story stone fireplace. A custom hand-woven Tibetan carpet from Odegard warms the stone floor. The drop-leaf trestle sofa table from Wright Table Company is used for books and games and is the perfect perch for a vintage rooster weather vane, *below*.

THE GARDEN ROOM IS A TRANQUIL RETREAT LOOKING OUT

onto the pool area and surrounding woodlands. Nature is brought indoors with furnishings,
including African slate floors and an organic lamp table of bundled twigs from La Lune, which supports a lamp
made from an old wallpaper roller, *facing*. ▪ The keeping room nestled in a niche outside the
kitchen is a quiet spot for a cup of coffee. The antique pine French daybed is accented with a nineteenth-century
Boutis quilt. The nineteenth-century oil painting appropriately depicts a mother and child cooking.
One of a set of four original Wallace Nutting ladder-back chairs is pulled up to an old French iron garden table, just
the spot to read recipes and the paper while waiting for a cake to bake, *above*.

THE MASTER SUITE was given an air of the French countryside with a beamed mansard ceiling and café au lait French toile, "Voyage En Chine," from Old World Weavers used on the walls as well as for bed hangings and curtains. The fireplace from Stone Magic was stained with tea bags to add age and patina, *left.* ▪ Ceiling beams reclaimed from a midwestern barn add architectural character and also help save trees. The cupola bed is enclosed with "Voyage En Chine" toile curtains and lined with a contrasting check from Pierre Frey; the curtains are hung by straps of "Contentin" from Lelievre, also used for banding the busy pattern. The bed coverlet, "La Bussiere," is also from Pierre Frey. The swing-arm reading lamps are by Christopher Norman.

*E*very detail counts in this inviting guest bedroom upholstered in Morris's "Pink and Rose"—each pleat of the bed skirt has its own flower. A soft, plaid area rug in stony beiges and forest greens from Elizabeth Eakins adds visual contrast. The "Trefoil" ottoman from O. Henry House provides extra seating next to the fireplace.

The guest bath is a lofty "tree house," with a pleasing mix of patterns, including "Acorn" wallpaper from Rose Cummings on the walls, a flooring grid work of four-inch African slate and Pratt & Larson tiles with acorns and oak leaves, *facing*. ▪ Leaves blown in from the garden are scattered between an antique owl humidor, an inkwell and a carved squirrel lamp in the guest bedroom, adding to the woodlands appeal, *left*. ▪ The powder room off the main entry is a secret grotto with walls covered in African slate slabs accented by a gilded, Empire wall mirror. The cast-stone sink from Renaissance is fitted with a Waterworks wall-mounted faucet set, *below*.

Barry's Tips

- Think hospitality before formality in the entry; invite guests inside with an appealing bench.

- Employ a kitchen designer to get the most of the space, then finish with your own choices of accessories and detailing.

- Mix masculine and feminine elements in a master bedroom suite so both husband and wife feel at home—for example, masculine, natural woods combine well with pretty French toiles.

- Sneak in a sofa or reading area if a hallway is generously proportioned.

- To maximize the use of a living room, make it multipurpose—study, library, music room and light dining or board games all in one room.

PALM BEACH PANACHE

Eighteenth-century stone pedestals hold luminaires strung with bamboo and seedpods rather than crystals, while an antique Murano glass chandelier hangs overhead. The blue-green Fortuny draperies were overpainted with metallic gold and shimmer like the scales of a fish.

MUSTIQUE IS A PRIVATE ISLAND in the French Caribbean, a tropical paradise of luxuriously appointed villas set amongst palm trees high above the sandy white beaches and clear blue ocean waters. After vacationing there for several winters with Barry, the owners asked him to plan a winter home of their own for them. Barry had already designed previous residences for the couple in Delaware and Maryland so knew just where to begin. It had to be in a sunny locale similar to the Caribbean but more accessible, somewhere in the States that was easy to slip away to for a long weekend. A place with style and sophistication, even a dash of flamboyance. Florida's sunny Palm Beach fit the bill precisely, and a large, waterfront lot was located not far from Worth Avenue and its charismatic winter social scene.

Influenced by the great 1940s English set designer and decorator Oliver Messel, an eccentric and larger-than-life persona known for his colorful and theatrical villas on Barbados, Mustique and other Caribbean islands, Barry incorporated dramatic designs of his own throughout the home. A hand-painted underwater mural in the dining room, a fantastic grotto powder room entirely covered in shells, and a striking open staircase spiraling upwards from a gurgling pool in the foyer became cornerstones of the project. Hand-mixed terrazzo floors in colors of sea green, sand, turquoise and raisin were used throughout to keep the floors cool to the touch, while twelve-foot ceilings helped circulate the warm air. Views were emphasized, and an infinity pool across the back merged the house into the ocean and sky.

The entry set a dramatic tone, with a spiraling staircase rising like a waterspout from a circular pool in the foyer. A wire mesh pedestal of Barry's design seems to float on the water's surface, supporting a large antique lead finial guiding the eye upward to the top of the stairwell, which was capped by a plaster domed ceiling. Constructed of overlapping fish scales, each individually cast by hand, the dome was illuminated by a midcentury glass-and-bronze chandelier that was found in Paris. Hand-cast undulating iron stair railings were highlighted against the walls, which were painted in Farrow & Ball cool white "Pointing."

At the top of the stairs, the second-floor mezzanine became an art and sculpture gallery with an organic collection from around the world—a large antique Asian drum as a center table, with a crusty nineteenth-century bust of Neptune surveying the quirky assemblage, including a trio of hanging leaded spheres (originally a Victorian English pawnshop sign) hanging overhead like giant South Sea pearls and a pair of ornately carved imbuya wood African doors mounted on the wall. Comfortable seating includes a tan leather settee and a modern Italian reed

The upper mezzanine seen from the guest suite shows tropical glamour at its best, as organic forms are deftly mixed with classical furnishings. The dramatic entry sweeps up the staircase with a vortex beginning with an antique lead finial in the entry. The domed ceiling is made of hand-applied fish scales lit by a mid-century modern chandelier found in Paris. The iron stair railings are custom made.

lounge chair set around a polished aluminum tea table. Shimmering silk Fortuny drapes in marine blues, greens and silvery golds luxuriously cascade onto the aqua blue terrazzo tiles, elegantly absorbing sound from the cool, uncarpeted floors.

The master suite opens off the mezzanine and overlooks the ocean. Much like a mystical Atlantis, the room was made

to glow with a watery blue sheen, the ceiling and Venetian plastered walls painted in misty Farrow & Ball sky-colored "Borrowed Light," while silk colonnades of hand-silk-screened aqua and taupe "China Seas" from Quadrille were hung across the windows and enveloped the bed. A striking, custom headboard was made from a nineteenth-century Tunisian wedding garment that is elaborately covered in hand-stitched tendrils of silver metallic threads and accented by a warm, sand-colored woven silk and cotton bed coverlet from Quadrille. An eighteenth-century Italian Carrera marble fireplace on the opposite wall with a midcentury-style chaise placed in front balanced the room, making a perfect spot for evening naps by the fire as the sun sets over the water. A neo-Baroque, white lacquered occasional chair (one of a pair) was placed in front of the windows. The adjoining sitting room continued with more exotic furnishings: an inlaid, Syrian center tabouret made of mother-of-pearl, camel bone and cedar; Barry's sensual "Odalisque" sofa upholstered in a soft, currant-colored linen; and an iron custom "Greek Key" lamp table in the corner. Motifs from the draperies were deftly repeated throughout the room for subtle visual interest and delight—the crisscross grid in the chinoiserie design, for example, was

continued on page 144

PRECEDING OVERLEAF: The master bedroom has the glow of an undersea cavern, its Venetian plaster walls and ceiling painted in pale blue Farrow & Ball "Borrowed Light." Shimmery "China Seas" turquoise linen draperies from Quadrille frame both the windows and the bed and help soften the carpetless floors. The eighteenth-century fireplace is Carrera marble.

A STRIKING HEADBOARD was custom designed from a nineteenth-century embroidered silk Tunisian wedding garment. The headboard's undulating form was inspired by the waves of the sea, *above left*. ▪ Subtle repetition of form is a cornerstone of Barry's design philosophy. Here the velvet-covered foot of the custom bed is echoed by the gilded lion's paw on the antique Italian nightstand behind. The sea blues and greens of the terrazzo floors are also repeated in the silk drapery panels, *below left*. ▪ The sitting room adjoining the master bedroom is a favorite spot to read and watch the fire. Color and designs in the draperies inspired the room's other furnishings—mother-of-pearl tabourets with crisscross patterns in their sides, a turquoise pillow on the "Odalesque" sofa from Tomlinson covered in raisin-colored linen. Barry also custom colored the iron Greek key lamp table resting in the corner, *facing*.

Her dressing room and the bath beyond are connected by a dramatic vestibule capped with a barrel-vaulted Venetian plaster ceiling. Watercolors from the 1930s of Adrian costume designs hang above the wrought-iron demilune French console. The zebra ottoman is an amusing yet graphic accent. The bath is anchored by an ample enameled Waterworks soaking tub. Note the tall cherry column on the side, which rotates to reveal hidden storage, FACING PAGE.

echoed in the carved side panel of a second smaller tabouret as well as on the arms of the lacquered occasional chair nearby.

The master suite runs the length of the second floor with spacious his and her dressing rooms and baths. An arresting groin-vaulted ceiling lit by a blown-glass Moorish lantern added a note of Mediterranean mystique to her dressing area and seductively leads the eye forward. Light streams into the bath from French doors off a private balcony, highlighting the sensuous enameled soaking tub. A tall, hollow lime-washed-cherry revolving column to the side of the tub was fitted with shelves for towels, while an Art Deco, smoked glass and crystal dressing screen reflected more angles of light back into the room. The light blue walls and blue-green terrazzo floors were accented with an elegant opaline blue table lamp and a powder blue velvet hassock set at the bronze and marble-topped Deco-style dressing table.

A second guest bedroom suite across the mezzanine was centered on a handsome gilt bronze canopy bed that was draped with horsehair linen panels of Scalamandré "Dogwood," the delicate linen blossoms used to upholster the walls for the light and airy look of an early morning Southern garden.

Designed as a potential full-time residence, two main-level guest suites were included. In one, a large Barbizon-style gilded mirror was leaned casually against the wall to reflect the furnishings back into the room. An ornately carved eighteenth-century French *canope au lit*, accented by an undulating, wavelike headboard below was covered in aqua green velvet. An Indian inlaid recamier was upholstered in coral and sand ribbed velvet, and an antique Italian carved gilt table rests nearby. Windowsills in this room, as throughout the house, were made of hand-cut coral stone to bring the actual texture of an ocean reef into the home.

Treasures of the deep were brought further indoors with a very special powder room off the foyer. Completely covered from floor to ceiling in swirling, hand-set patterns of seashells, it is Sinbad's secret grotto beneath the waves. It took artisan Cathy Jarman more than three weeks to install, using hundreds of sparkling and iridescent shells—oyster, clam, abalone and cowry, turkey wing and comb, as well as coral and sea glass. A cast-stone sink and an antique carved and gilded mirror above seem to float within the fantastic seashell reef.

Entering the dining room is like swimming down into a Sargasso Sea. The walls and ceiling were covered in a hand-painted mural of shadowy underwater motifs. Forty-five-degree corners transformed the room into an intimate octagon, with the iridescent marine blue and khaki drapery panels of Osborne & Little "Coromandel" silk damask framing each corner as well as absorbing sounds from dining. An antique chandelier with a mercury glass orb was floated like a bubble above the table, which is made of two hand-forged iron pedestals in the form of large roots topped with a cool olive-and-tan cast-concrete oval. Nineteenth-century Venetian gilt chairs with their original crusty patina still intact were set around the table, their seats covered with yellow-green silk. Niches on either side of the room hold gilded nineteenth-century architectural columns that support large shell-encrusted urns. The overall effect is elegant dining twenty thousand leagues under the sea.

Several shallow, arched steps lead from the foyer down into the sunken living area, whose square shape was cleverly deconstructed with an elliptical trough of seashells inscribed within the perimeter of the ceiling, making the room appear oval. The three-dimensional molding was made by casting actual shells in plaster and the illusion continued by painting the inner ceiling sky blue, as if the room were open to the heavens. An antique

A downstairs guest suite is a portal into *a magic kingdom* seen through the large gilded mirror. The Indian recamier is upholstered in Osborne & Little ribbed velvet "Delamont," which highlights the mother-of-pearl inlay. Mist-colored sheers blow gently in the breeze between the drapery panels of Osborne & Little "Chrysanthe," also used on the antique French bed canopy, FACING PAGE.

Carrera marble fireplace guarded by mythical mock turtles on its sides is the room's focal point, with comfortable and movable furnishings grouped around: a club chair and ottoman upholstered in abalone and cream-blue jacquard, a lounge chair in a turquoise and tan silk damask, a curvilinear sofa upholstered in misty blue-green cotton. A spectacular, brilliantly sparkling chartreuse Murano glass chandelier became the room's crowning touch; custom made in Italy, it boasts gracefully winding and curving tendrils of glass, like a delicate flower from the depths of the sea.

Slabs of coral were used for windowsills throughout the house.

Adjacent to the living room is the library, a masculine retreat upholstered in a chocolate linen, which was repeated as the ground for curtains printed with Quadrille "China Seas." A custom-designed system of open, bronze wall shelving and a nineteenth-century iron and oak drafting table at the window rather than a traditional desk gave the room an early industrial air, as did a pair of adjustable iron floor lamps. An L-shaped "Robertson" sofa designed by Barry for Tomlinson and upholstered in Donghia "Krazy Quilt" matelasse in pleasing aqua green was accented with cocoa and cream banding.

The kitchen and family room open off the opposite side of the living room. Much like a laboratory, the SieMatic kitchen is cool and to the point with stone countertops, wooden cabinets lacquered in a pale seafoam green, and copper pendant lights hanging like work lights over the center island. Industrial nickel-plated appliances are appropriate accents. In the pantry, an early-twentieth-century gymnasium locker was used for storage.

An open, casual dining space rests between the kitchen and the family room, which was set across the back overlooking a covered loggia, fireplace and infinity pool. An unusual coffee table constructed from an industrial, welded-iron panel centers the comfortable seating arrangement of Barry's "Marche" sofa covered in a pale tan suede, handsome "Boomerang" chairs highlighted with cerused oak detailing, and an Arts and Crafts bench below the television (hidden behind a folding screen of hand-colored eighteenth-century tropical engravings). Osborne & Little "Pera" linen draperies with an abstract African design line the French doors opening to the loggia and shield the room from the strong Florida sun.

Beautiful, colorful and refreshingly tropical, the home is just what the owners had in mind—their own Caribbean paradise in Palm Beach.

The dining room's hand-painted mural by Warnock Studios on the walls and ceiling suggests shadowy, mysterious ocean depths. Niches across two corners help transform the room into a cozy octagon. Osborne & Little "Coromandel" silk damask draperies help absorb sound and add to the room's glamorous intimacy, *facing*. ▪ Textures and forms subtly weave a tapestry in the living room with an antique, crusty iron table pulled up to the curvilinear sofa covered in cotton, *above left*. ▪ The vestibule leading from the study to the living room is softened by an archway; a Moroccan light adds an exotic glow overhead, *above right*.

A secret grotto, the powder room is completely encrusted with seashells from floor to ceiling. Many were gathered locally, including hundreds of oyster shells from local restaurants. The stone sink is from Stoneyard and bronze wall sconces from Robert Abbey, *above left*. ▪ Actual seashells were cast in resin molds and made into a trough around the ceiling to help de-emphasize the room's square contours, *above right*. ▪ A cast oval inset of seashells around the perimeter of the ceiling helps distract the eye from the room's square contours. A curvilinear sofa in pale blue and green cotton adds to the fluidity. The overmantel mirror from Dennis & Leen reflects light back into the space. Terrazzo floors are kept bare throughout the house for coolness, *facing*.

*A*ndalusian-inspired turquoise front doors welcome visitors into the entrance foyer, which steps down to the living room beyond. A limestone-topped table is complemented with mobile wedge ottomans for drinks and conversation. Note the original crusty blue surface of the antique wrought-iron wall console, *facing.* ▪ The library was conceived as a more masculine workspace set with a nineteenth-century drafting table overlooking the pool and ocean. Scientific-looking floor lamps add to the impression. Storage boxes for files were placed beneath the windows, and a custom-designed wall shelving system provides ample room for books and collections, *above.*

*L*acquered cabinets in pale seafoam green with long, nickel-plated handles and straightforward stone counters lend the air of a laboratory to the kitchen. Note the vintage French gym locker used for additional storage. Blenko glass decanters from the 1960s add a colorful accent, *facing left*. ▪ An open kitchen shelf displays a playful mélange of bowls, a reflection of the masterful mix of elements throughout the house, including a pair of eighteenth-century French open-weave iron baskets, a Deco ceramic mixing bowl with a pouring spout and contemporary woks, *facing right*. ▪ An informal dining area separates the kitchen from the family room, and portieres help screen off the area when needed. Hammered-copper lights overhead unify the two spaces. Chairs around the radial table are covered in rope for a maritime accent. Kitchen cabinets are from SieMatic, *above*.

THE FAMILY ROOM OVERLOOKS THE LOGGIA AND POOL.

Cerused oak chairs of Barry's design are grouped around his "Le Marche" sofa and a "Michael" bench below the flat-screen
television (discreetly covered with hinged panels of Asian engravings when not in use).
Christian Liagre open bookcases flank the bench and display collections of maritime books and artifacts.

Barry's Tips

- Take a design element from a fabric and repeat it in other mediums for visual coordination and appeal: in the master bedroom/sitting room a crisscross grid from a drapery panel was subtly repeated on a side table and chair.

- Make a square room appear oval by inscribing the ceiling with an elegant oval band or molding.

- Bring inspiration from the sea indoors—actual coral for the windowsills can be a striking tropical accent.

- Make a room more intimate by taking out the corners. Here the dining room was made into an inviting octagon by eliminating the corners with draperies and niches.

- Let your imagination run wild in a small powder room and cover it from top to bottom with shells, fabric or an arresting mural.

TROPICAL COLOR IN A CARIBBEAN VILLA

An escape from the tropical heat, the living room is cool and restful, centered with a "Michael" bench and matching pair of sofas (through Tomlinson). Simple wicker chairs and a sea grass carpet add to the relaxed island atmosphere.

THE OWNERS OF THIS Caribbean villa had been wintering in St. Bart's for several years. Enchanted with the climate and tropical setting, they were delighted when they were able to acquire a small villa perched on a mountaintop high above the ocean. While the setting was spectacular, with sweeping views of the rocky island slopes and azure blue waters of the Caribbean below, the house was more than thirty years old and needed significant updating. Rooms were poorly configured, small and dark (the living room ceiling, for example, had been stained an unappealing muddy brown).

Barry, who had been raised abroad in tropical settings such as New Caledonia and South Africa, understood what was required: the villa needed to be opened up to the brilliant Caribbean sunshine and the surrounding vistas to celebrate its dramatic mountaintop setting. The owners and French architect Pierre Monsaingeon were involved in every phase of the planning and construction process, and there were frequent meetings both in St. Bart's and back home in the United States.

Wiring, plumbing and lighting were updated under the island's strict energy and building codes, which required working within the original structural framework of the house. Windows and doors were enlarged, letting in the sunlight and breezes—fresh mountain mists in the morning and cool, fragrant zephyrs rising off the sea in the evening. The colors of the tropics were brought indoors with bright greens and sunny chartreuses, along with richly saturated turquoises and blue greens. An infinity pool was added across the back of the house to transition from the home to the surroundings. New bedrooms for visiting family and guests were constructed, each with its own bath, and the galley kitchen was enlarged and updated. It wasn't long before a

new villa began to emerge from its former shell, captivating all who entered with its colorful Caribbean charm and impossibly perfect views.

The living area remained the center of the house. Wide glass hurricane doors that fold and disappear into the walls were added across the back and side, flooding the room with sunlight and spectacular views. Because window and door heights could not be raised due to building code restrictions, smoky mirrored-glass transoms were installed above to reflect an illusion of height back into the room. Walls were painted a clean linen white and spaces were kept open with a breakfast and drinks pass-through bar off the adjoining kitchen.

Designed for both large parties as well as small family gatherings, the room was balanced with a handsome Arts and Crafts–inspired "Michael" bench in the center and matching "Michael" sofas across either side of the room. The sofas, part of Barry's collection for Tomlinson, were upholstered in a pale blue brushed linen to reflect the colors of the sky and water. A trio of custom-designed backless bar stools at the pass-through bar were covered in durable aqua chenille "Doge" from Osborne & Little. A wing chair covered in "Boxwood Stripe" cotton from Sister Parrish added a less traditional, more informal accent, while the turquoise Quadrille "Paradise" linen print was chosen for the draperies, their soft folds gently blowing in the Caribbean breezes. A "Large Cubic" bronze lantern from Formations was placed overhead, providing a geometric counterweight for the angles of the room. Entertainment systems—television and stereos—were subtly camouflaged within a mesh corner pedestal; the screen can be deftly hidden behind the draperies when not in use.

To maximize space, a loft was carved out below the eaves and accessed by an open staircase; a combination study and

A simple white caned chair rests against the sea-blue-green walls of the pantry, the tropical colors inspired by the Caribbean island setting.

bedroom for two, with twin British Khaki daybeds, it is now a favorite hideaway for grandchildren, kept open and light but still private with a scrim of sheers in "Vivace" from Creation Baumann.

Additional living space was created by accessing the large verandas that wrap around the back and side of the house. The overhanging roof was extended and softened with striped awnings in colors of the island—kiwi, olive and deep turquoise—the colorful canvas shades also providing much-needed protection from the strong afternoon sun. Teak (cooler to lie on) replaced the former concrete decks, and 1,200 square feet of shimmering blue glass mosaic tiles were imported for an infinity pool that seems to flow off into the sky. An octagonal cabana was added at the south end of the deck, becoming the perfect spot for watching the sunset while nestled amongst piles of colorful cushions and aqua blue upholstered seats on the built-in banquette. Hardy sheers of oyster-colored "Shimmer" from Perennials were hung on rings and pulled back to prevent them blowing in the tropical breezes. And on the north corner of the deck, a teak trestle dining table was placed for magical al fresco dining high above the ocean, set with wrought-iron chairs and lit by an exotic Moroccan lantern flickering overhead.

The galley kitchen was widened to make it easier to use and a fountain was installed just outside the jalousie window, the gurgling water psychologically cooling the cooks inside. Walls and ceiling were painted a cool aquamarine blue and teak cabinets were installed for a tailored, shipshape smartness. Even the La Cornue range was enameled in a deep and soothing cerulean blue.

The usable space of the main-floor master suite, which looks out to the pool, was extended outdoors by the addition of

LOOKING TOWARD the outdoor decks, the cabana is glimpsed on the right. A walnut center table holds philodendron leaves gathered from the garden, while a planter makes a handy basket for pool towels. Turquoise linen curtains frame the view.

The upstairs loft doubles as a study and extra bedroom. It is furnished with a pair of daybeds upholstered in "Mangrove Woven Stripe" from Brunschwig & Fils

a private sitting room on the terrace created with a pair of small sofas. Even though this is a vacation home, beautiful textiles were used throughout to emphasize a feeling of luxury—a green and tan "Aspley" rug from Stark Carpet was complemented by Bergamo "Lana Reversible" white linen panels on the four-poster bed and windows. The master bath was planned to allow glimpses of the sea while showering, an oyster-colored Roman shade of indoor-outdoor fabric adding privacy.

The first-floor guest suite was painted the color of a melon from the local market—a lively chartreuse—and complementary fabrics were chosen, including a "Skukusa" green-on-cream bed coverlet from Sister Parrish and "Roxanne" striped aqua and olive throw pillows from Boussac. A tall, open "Loire" iron canopy bed from Niermann Weeks was found to add a note of architectural drama in the otherwise simple room. A green lacquered desk was placed in front of the window, which was framed by curtains in kiwi and cream. (Jalousie windows were added across the entire house to add a note of cottage charm inspired by local island architecture.)

Downstairs three additional bedrooms with their own baths were created in bright and cool palettes of morning yellows and tropical blues. Furnishings were kept open and comfortable—a four-poster "Chelmsford Bamboo" bed and a caned "Sarazin" lounge chair from British Khaki in one bedroom, along with a cream-and-white-striped sofa bed for relaxed seating while watching the bright green parrots frolic in the banana trees outside.

Inviting, colorful and yet well suited for everyday living, the villa now aptly reflects the beauty of its tropical setting, truly one of the most beautiful places on earth.

and a table for games and studies with versatile seating, including ottomans upholstered in "Apple" blue linen from Sister Parrish, *facing*. ▪ Japanese raku pots line the shelf above the open kitchen pass-through. The bar stools were custom designed to be comfortable and backless so as to keep the view unobstructed while being sturdy enough to not tip over easily. The front door is visible to the left of the kitchen, *below*.

𝒜 drinks and serving bar is set on the potting console, designed by Barry, on the side deck. Functioning awnings were found locally, *above*. Blue mosaic tiles in the infinity pool reflect the clear blue sky as the sun rises over the beach. Chaises are covered in "Bikini Stripe" from Giati, *facing above*. ▪ Ready for a romantic evening, cobalt blue votive bottles rest on the potting trough console on the terrace, *facing below*.

The view while seated in the cabana looking across the infinity pool into the harbor below is breathtaking. Shimmer curtains remain outdoors year-round fitted with Haas's silk brocade "Aristeo," which is complemented by the curving "Westminster" chenille banding from Gisbert Rentmeister on the sea grass carpet, *above left*. ▪ In the living room, drapery

pulls are straightforward—bamboo rods with decorative wrought-iron handles. Note the curtain lining is simply tied to the draperies to avoid shrinkage from moisture and subsequent puckering,

facing below. ▪ An octagonal cabana tucked into the corner of the deck makes a cozy spot for drinks and watching the sunsets. A stone table is flanked by a wrought-iron chair. Fabrics include

pillows in teal and yellow "Banu" from Creation Baumann, "Beachside Stripe" from Giati on the bench and oyster-colored "Tanglewood" (through Nomi) on the chair and pillows.

*J*alousie windows were added across the house to complement local architecture, *below*. ▪ The galley kitchen was updated with new appliances, teak cabinets and aggregate puce-colored countertops. A Roman shade made from soft blue "Boxwood Stripe" from Sister Parrish shades the sink, which overlooks a softly gurgling fountain in front of the house, *facing above*. ▪ The trestle dining table from Sutherland lets diners look out over the island and sandy beaches below. "Bikini Stripe" fabric from Giati softens the wrought-iron Janus et Cie chairs, while boiserie candelabras lend an exotic air, *facing below*.

canopy bed in the master bedroom is hung with Bergamo "Lana Reversible" sheer; the geometry of its design is repeated in the bench at the foot of the bed and in the textured wool carpet, *above left*. ▪ An antique oval mirror reflects the comfortable and inviting guest bedroom, *above right*. ▪ The low-ceilinged downstairs guest bedroom reflects the inviting palette of soft banana cream walls and tall furnishings that were deliberately chosen to accentuate a feeling of height, including a "Chelmsford Bamboo" bed from British Khaki, which is covered with a linen coverlet in "Norcombe Hill" from Osborne & Little, *facing*.

The master dressing room and bath features a walk-in shower overlooking the pool and deck. The Roman shade in the shower is made from moisture-resistant indoor-outdoor fabric. A bamboo and rattan chest provides storage, *facing*. ▪ The guest bedroom was painted in a warm Caribbean chartreuse and furnished with a tall canopy bed to exaggerate the room's height. The living room and breakfast bar are glimpsed beyond the open door. Framed collections of shells on the wall add to the island ambience, *left*. ▪ A green lacquered writing desk sits at the window and holds a colorful assortment of tropical blooms, *below*.

Barry's Tips

- A small room with low ceilings becomes larger when both walls and ceiling are painted one enveloping color—for example, a small guest room completely covered in cheerful chartreuse expands and blurs its boundaries.

- Tie curtain linings to the outer panels rather than sewing them together to avoid shrinkage and puckering in humid climates.

- Use indoor-outdoor fabric on window shades in a shower or bath to screen the window and repel moisture and mildew.

- When furnishing a large room several versions of the same piece make the space more cohesive—a pair of "Michael" sofas along with a coordinating bench in the center unite the open living room.

- Use native colors to relate to a locale—here tropical hues of kiwi and chartreuse, soft, creamy banana, aqua turquoise and ocean blue were combined for a colorful, Caribbean palette.

TOTIER
CREEK FARM

The entry hall stretches the width of the house. Woodwork is painted in Farrow & Ball "String," which accents the original heart pine floors. A glass Vaughn "pumpkin" lantern at the rear adds a soft glow, *facing*. ▪ Brunschwig & Fils documentary wallpaper "Maize" is used in the entry hall and stairwell, *above*.

NOT MUCH HAS CHANGED in the bucolic countryside of central Virginia over the past 300 years. One of the last undeveloped areas of the Eastern Seaboard, the softly rolling hills of Albemarle County are still dotted with Colonial-era plantations and estates, including historic Totier Creek Farm. Built in 1760 (and remodeled in 1798 following a fire), the wooden frame farmhouse is set on a gently rising knoll with sweeping views of the countryside. While enlarged in the mid-nineteenth century, the farm's Colonial-era character was carefully kept intact, including wide-plank heart pine floors, several fine Federal-era mantels and even the original front door and brass hardware.

When the current owners purchased the property, they were looking for a quiet retreat, something with character and charm and away from urban crowds. Although the house was structurally sound, it had had "improvements" over time that needed to be remedied: wide, 1950s windows needed replacing with the eighteenth-century nine-over-six sashes originally used in the house; handsome paneling in the study needed conserving and restoring in a more period-appropriate palette; and the kitchen, although remodeled, was not in keeping with the rest of the home and required a redesign. At the same time, the old colonial needed to be brought forward for twenty-first-century living with updated baths and family areas for visiting children and guests.

Working with architect Bahlmann Abbot, Barry approached the process carefully, recognizing the need to preserve as much of the home's original character as possible, refreshing the interiors but within the parameters of a graceful yet unpretentious country farmhouse. Original hardware was

oldest section of the early colonial home
and is furnished with inviting seating around the fireplace.
An armchair on the left is covered in vine and leaf
woven brocade. A braided sisal carpet anchors the room.

conserved and matched with modern reproductions, stair spindles and stringers were methodically stripped and freshened with a coat of new paint, and period mantels and fireplaces were repointed and restored. A warren of bedrooms on the second floor was sensitively consolidated into a master suite—the bath and dressing room with commanding views of the countryside—but without altering the original upstairs hall and room layouts. Simple and welcoming, the house began to shine with an understated elegance, a reflection of not only its past but also its future.

The center hall runs the length of the house front to back and is the heart of the home. Light streams in from both ends—over the original transoms above the front door as well as from the dining room windows at the rear—filling the hall with a soft glow that bounces off the gleaming heart pine floors. Brunschwig & Fils golden and cream "Maize" wallpaper was chosen—with its swans, swags and palmettes mixed with corn and wheat stalks—to reflect eighteenth-century classicism as well as the countryside. The handsome stair woodwork was detailed with Farrow & Ball "String" and "New White" to complement the wallpaper. French doors and sidelights were added to close off the dining room when division of the public and private spaces was desired.

Opening off the entry, the library's original eighteenth-century paneled walls were glazed with a rich colonial olive "Calke Green" from Farrow & Ball to emphasize its classic character. One of the oldest rooms in the house, it was made warm and welcoming with a pair of comfortable sofas upholstered in a gold and cream figured velvet. A relaxing lounge chair and ottoman covered in a Watts of Westminster over-scaled Federal green chenille damask, as well as a button-tufted green suede ottoman, were set in front of the fireplace to add to the room's soft and inviting charm. Bookcases along the wall were lined with Donghia raffia, as was the ceiling for more intimacy, and the shelving was highlighted with handsome brass tacks. Printed linen curtains from Raoul Textiles in walnut, olive and café au lait envelop the room in their soft folds.

continued on page 186

AN EIGHTEENTH-CENTURY oil of a young girl eating fruit centers the opposite wall, *above left*. ▪ The family room opens off the kitchen and is comfortably furnished with a London sofa and a pair of "Plantation" lounge chairs from Hickory Chair. An antique bench with a tan suede top doubles as a coffee table. The Palladian cabinets were built to hide the bar and television. The open kitchen and dining room are seen beyond, *center left*. ▪ A Georgian glass compote is filled with fresh eggs from the farm, while

a nineteenth-century ceramic hen rests
behind. The table is set with a service
of Wedgwood creamware that dates
from the late eighteenth century, *facing
below.* ▪ The dining room is surrounded
by vistas of the countryside that inspired
the colors in the room. Walls are upholstered in Donghia's wheat-colored raffia
and simple window treatments are constructed with Brunschwig & Fils "The
Walnut Tree" cotton print. A nineteenth-
century French walnut semainier on the
back wall holds linens, with a drawer for
each day of the week. A combination
of chairs and fabrics are used for more
individuality: at the antique dining
table, Rose Tarlow buttermilk-washed
"Chippendale" side chairs are mixed
with host and hostess chairs upholstered
in Brunschwig & Fils "Elba Woven"
stripe, *above.*

OVERLEAF: In the music room, windows are softened with panels of "Pashmina" (Thomas Dare) to muffle sound and complement the original heart pine floors. Walls are painted with Farrow & Ball "String." An iron boiserie lantern from Formations hangs over a center table draped with a crewel linen. Four Hickory Chair lattice-back chairs with buttermilk wash provide movable seating for musical soirees. The cased glass-front hutch in the corner is Barry's design through David Iatesta and was inspired by an English antique.

A ROUNDED CORNER cabinet displays more creamware in a corner of the dining room, *facing*. ▪ Andy Warhol's silkscreen of Uncle Sam rests on the mantel, its bright colors complemented with an Early American quilt for a sophisticated mélange of old and new. The mantel's elliptical and radial designs are repeated in the antique circular sconces above, as well as a pair of Victorian Indian clubs on the sofa table across the room, *above*. ▪ The family's golden retriever enjoys a nap on the "London" sofa from R. Jones, *above right*. ▪ Kitchen cabinets are constructed in limed oak on top and washed with buttermilk tones below. Concrete countertops are a soft mushroom color, and walls are tiled with acid-etched stone that is decorated with country herbs. The book stand, earthenware egg dish and amber glass canister jar are antiques; eggs are from hens raised on the farm, *right*.

The gentle curves of a *Venetian fruitwood bench* at the foot of the bed are echoed in the custom headboard inspired by a garden bench from Janus et Cie. Barry designed a tole cresting to accent the canopy and gave it a cream wash with gilt highlights, colors reflecting the cornstalks on the hall wallpaper, FACING PAGE.

At the end of the hall, the light-filled dining room overlooks vistas of the surrounding hills and farms. Window treatments were kept simple so as not to detract from the views, with panels of Brunschwig & Fils "The Walnut Tree" cotton print in cream, cocoa, terra-cotta and soft blue green—the colors of eggs collected each morning from the farm's henhouse. Quiet and understated furnishings were chosen in keeping with the farm's humble origins: an early-nineteenth-century Federal dining table lit by a green patinated iron and wood "Gustavian" chandelier from Dennis & Leen and unassuming "Chippendale" side chairs from Rose Tarlow, simply yet elegantly upholstered in Fortuny rose damask. An elliptical corner cabinet displays part of a large collection of eighteenth-century Wedgwood creamware used for dinner parties, and next to it a small, antique mahogany side table is set for tea, paired with a comfortable "Spencer" wing chair and "Ryan" sofa from George Smith covered in Brunschwig & Fils "Tatiana," a figured buttercup plaid.

The adjoining kitchen had been remodeled but with modern products incongruent with a simple farmhouse; so it was sensitively brought back to a more appropriate ambience with kitchen designer Lois Kennedy. Handcraftsmanship was emphasized, with a combination of limed oak upper cabinets and lower cupboards washed with soft buttermilk paint. Mushroom-colored concrete counters were a practical as well as aesthetic touch. Walls were covered with warm gray stone tiles, used floor to ceiling for straightforwardness of material as well as ease of maintenance. A family keeping room centered on a handsome Victorian copy of a Federal mantel was added beyond the kitchen; unabashedly modern with a television and French doors opening to a terrace and pool, it is a favorite spot while meals are prepared. The citrus limes and yellows of an Andy Warhol silkscreen on the mantel are reflected in a simple antique American quilt laid across the back of the sofa, a subtle reminder that modern elements can be successfully incorporated in period interiors when linked by color and pattern.

Upstairs, several small rooms across the back of the house were consolidated into a handsome master suite, dressing room and interconnecting bath. The soft tones of the harvest fields were brought back into the room—golden wheat, maize, dreamy white cotton—with Hodsoll McKenzie linen "Tulip Bouquet," which was used to upholster the walls as well as for draperies and the half-tester bed. Cream-and-gold "Floral Check" linen, also from Hodsoll McKenzie, on the inner canopy curtains was continued in the dressing room, where it was used for Roman shades as well as ceiling and wall coverings to subtly tie the adjoining rooms together. A tall Swedish-type cabinet with oversized bun feet and mirrored doors was designed to reflect the light and views back into the dressing room as well as add additional natural light for dressing. A round, tufted ottoman centered the room, and a custom-built bench and window seat looks out at the original 1760 farmhouse, now restored as guest quarters and offices. Charles Dana Gibson prints on the wall reference the famous illustrator, who was a neighbor and frequent guest in the early twentieth century.

Additional guest rooms, each with their own fireplaces and baths, include a very feminine suite for a visiting daughter and friends. Canopy beds are draped with Brunschwig & Fils "Ode to Spring" in aquas, pinks and creams, pleasingly contrasted with "Otello" a lively cream-and-rouge large plaid from Boussac used for inner curtains and the headboards. The curves of a custom channel-back chair and ottoman upholstered in Breton red "Antigonas" from Fonthill were repeated in a glazed terra-cotta garden seat used as a side table. A contemporary abstract oil painting and collection of modern glass vases on the eighteenth-century serpentine chest echo the blue greens and faded flag reds of the fabrics in the room, while adding a pleasing modern accent.

A spring palette of soft vernal greens and creams was the inspiration for the second guest bedroom. Kathryn Ireland's "Paisley Stripe" was used for the bed hangings, coverlet and

window draperies, along with her tender "Floral Green" linen print, used not only for inner canopy curtains and bed pillows but also paper backed and applied as wall covering to evoke the romance of a garden bower. A comfortable "Freeman" chair and ottoman from Hickory Chair next to the Federal mantel covered in Hodsoll McKenzie "Large Linen Check" is a favorite spot for reading novels late at night by the fireplace.

The music room opens off the entry hall downstairs and was kept warm and inviting with a fall palette of amber, olive, almond and warm yellow, making a cozy retreat on a chilly winter evening. Drapery panels of Thomas Dare "Pashmina" from Donghia subtly absorb sounds during musical soirees held at the baby grand piano. A center table was draped with "Jardin De Fantasie," a crewel wool and linen from Fonthill, to further soften the room, and an iron boiserie lantern overhead was added for a romantic accent. Several collections were displayed in the room, including one of multihued art glass lamp shades in the cased glass hutch that Barry designed.

History is kept alive at Totier Creek Farm through a judicious blend of old and new, its past honored and sensitively reinterpreted for modern living.

In the new dressing room, the big bun feet of the Swedish-style armoire lift it off the floor, while mirrored panels telescope light and space back into the room. The round shape of the tufted ottoman is reinforced with a round rug that helps to break up the otherwise square room. Hodsoll McKenzie "Floral Check" is used for the walls and ceiling, as well as the Roman shade, for an intimate and cozy appeal, *facing left*. ▪ One of the farm's original eighteenth-century buildings can be glimpsed from the window seat, *facing right*.
▪ The master bedroom is a dreamy haven of honey, ivory and taupe with draperies of "Tulip Bouquet" (Hodsoll McKenzie through Zimmer & Rhode), also used to upholster the walls. The owner wanted a spot for tea in every room, and here a creamy pedestal tea table is flanked by a pair of tufted "Karin" chairs from O. Henry House. A "Summerfield White" carpet from Stark provides a pleasing neutral accent, *above*.

- Modern elements can be successfully incorporated in period interiors when linked by colors or patterns.

- Raffia is simple and unassuming, absorbs sounds and works well in a variety of interiors for both wall and ceiling coverings.

- When in the country bring it back inside—hues of the wheat and cornfields were reflected in the home's textiles and furnishings.

- When bare floors are present, drape tables to absorb sounds and soften the room.

- Personalize chairs and give them individuality by using different but complementary upholstery.

Color continues in the guest room with a faded Breton red lounge chair covered with Fonthill "Antigonas" floral, the perfect complement to feminine and pretty Brunschwig & Fils "Ode to Spring" linen

window curtains. The antique serpentine chest is freshened with contemporary art and glass vases on top, *facing.* ▪ Color and pattern are expertly combined in an upstairs guest bedroom whose walls are painted in soft blue Farrow & Ball "Borrowed Light," which complements the bed drapery. A custom homespun rug of ecru and Breton red stripes is a pleasing geometric accent. Walnut benches at the feet of the beds are upholstered in plaid linen "Otello" from Boussac, as are the headboards and interior bed curtains. The hand-tinted photograph between the beds is the owner's great-great-grandmother, *above.*

COMING
HOME TO
ELWAY HALL

A corner of the great hall is casually arranged for conversation, centered on a citrus-colored antique Oushak carpet. The room's formal molding was kept intact, underscored with Farrow & Ball "Lime White" on the walls and ceiling.

OVERLEAF: The great hall is divided from the entry by thin veils of sheer linen panels for more intimacy while leaving the historic home's original architecture intact. A gilded nineteenth-century eagle bookstand greets visitors on the washed-oak center table. Wire mesh pedestals are Barry's design for Darr George.

CHILDHOOD, THE EXPERTS SAY, is what shapes our taste as adults, and Barry readily admits this holds true for him. Raised in a gracious Southern manor and historic residences around the world, he grew up with tall ceilings, sweeping staircases, wide moldings, claw-foot tubs and fireplaces in nearly every room. The romance of traditional architecture with its proper scale and proportion never really left him, and when he came across an old Edwardian manor for sale in the western Virginia countryside, it was like coming back home.

Elway Hall had been built in 1907 by a wealthy industrialist as a wedding present for his daughter. When Barry viewed it almost a century later, the fourteen-foot ceilings, Tiffany stained and leaded glass windows, seventeen fireplaces and grand carved-oak staircase were all still intact. The 20,000-square-foot house, however, certainly needed work: the kitchen had been "modernized" and needed to be returned to a more appropriate Edwardian ambience; electrical and heating systems were out of date; and the large, public rooms required freshening and needed to be made more casual and inviting.

Barry began with the entry hall. Set with a sweeping oak staircase that opens into the great hall, the area was divided with translucent linen panels hung from the ceiling as scrims on simple wrought-iron rods—a clean and straightforward solution combining mystery and intimacy. Walls, ceilings and plasterwork were painted with Farrow & Ball chalky "Lime White" for a bright and unpretentious welcome and to highlight the natural waxed-oak woodwork of the door and window casings. A round, cerused-oak table placed in the center was chosen to focus the space.

The music and garden room glows with Farrow & Ball "Ciara Yellow" paint. The crusty eighteenth-century French armillary sphere once belonged to famous decorator Jacques Grange, as did the iron center table. A pair of folding Gothic screens in Brunschwig & Fils "Treillage" set in the windows highlight the view of the gardens, eliminating the need for drapery, FACING PAGE.

In the adjacent great hall, antiques and contemporary pieces were mixed together for inviting and versatile conversational arrangements. A tall, iron mesh pedestal designed by Barry, with a massive eighteenth-century leaded "Warrick" urn resting on top, holds court in the center of the room, while at the far end a comfortable sofa covered in a pale wheat and gold chenille damask anchors a collection of antique French, English and Italian chairs set in a loose radius around it. An antique Oushak carpet inspired the soft palette of orange, taupe and cream. Massive floor lamps on either end of the sofa were chosen as counterpoints for the eighteenth-century Italian giltwood tea table and tufted leather ottoman in front. Architectural treasures include a nineteenth-century faux marbleized wooden theatrical balustrade set as a console against one of the deep, oak windowsills that holds a collection of terracotta busts and antiques. Simple, unlined linen panels at the windows further de-emphasize the room's formality.

Inspired by Wedgwood Jasperware, Barry painted the music room walls and ceiling with Farrow & Ball glowing "Ciara Yellow" and highlighted the elaborate raised-plaster moldings with Farrow & Ball "New White." To give the feeling of both garden room and music room, furnishings are a mix of organic and traditional—a contemporary woven willow chair sits next to the old walnut Steinway, while Barry's comfortable, overstuffed "Odalesque" sofa rests in the broad bay window, flanked by a Victorian iron garden chair and an Edwardian button-tufted lounge chair. A twisting forged-iron center table and crusty eighteenth-century armillary set on a tall limestone column help enhance the feeling of an indoor garden. The bronze gas and electric chandelier is one of a pair and original to the room.

The library, opening off the music room, is a masculine retreat. Walls were painted in Farrow & Ball deep reddish brown "Mahogany," and the room was furnished with Gothic, Edwardian and Renaissance pieces: an antique red leather Chesterfield settee, a hooded English hall porter's chair, an oak daybed covered in ribbed brown velvet. Shelves of well-read books line one wall, while collections are displayed for observation and study around the room, including a large group of painstakingly labeled Victorian seashells mounted in shadowboxes hung together on a wall. An octagonal turret expands the corner and holds a group of antique globes set on a fin de siècle drafting table in the center.

The family room was made friendly and relaxing with an autumnal palette of reds, oranges and golds. Walls were covered with wheat-colored raffia and the ceiling was painted with cheerful Farrow & Ball "India Yellow." Overscaled accessories chosen for drama include a pair of large, lidded antique Moroccan jars on the mantel and a massive industrial gear. A loose but balanced and comfortable group of seating includes a skirted chair covered in a striking zigzag woven tapestry from Clarence House and a sofa in "Alladin" from Quadrille.

Barry started from scratch in the kitchen, taking out stainless steel appliances, glossy new cabinets and even recently laid hardwood floors that were much too shiny and new. With thoughts of the tiled William Morris Luncheon Rooms at the Victoria and Albert Museum in London, he chose Pratt and Larson tiles in hay and cream for the walls. The hand-fired tiles were accented with randomly placed, molded silhouettes of barnyard animals—geese, cows, sheep, pigs and turkeys, along with turnips, corn and wheat—for a look of country charm. The upper wall was papered in Morris's "Apple" in a custom block print, and this was carried onto the ceiling for a cozy, English touch.

The cabinets were crafted from quartersawn oak to expose their grain, then limed and waxed for a simple, honest

ECLECTIC OBJECTS RESTING ON
an architectural balustrade console and deep windowsill in
the living room include a pair of seventeenth-century
Tunisian marble vessels, French gold dore candlesticks and an
eighteenth-century Venetian damask coffer. Simple linen sheers
informally frame the windows.

finish. Splats were given a slight flair for a stronger silhouette, and overscaled, brass outer door hardware was chosen for the cabinet handles and pulls, for a heavier, handcrafted solidity. Memories of Maxfield Parrish's children's book illustrations guided the design of a free-hanging cabinet along one wall; made to look as if it were found and added separately, it was built with open racks for dishes and custom-blown imperfect glass doors and was painted a bittersweet orange, the color of a warm October afternoon.

The adjoining butler's pantry was converted into a breakfast nook with an L-shaped banquette built into the corner. Morris's "Apple" was continued on the walls in the same inviting autumn palette that Barry chose himself: Benjamin Moore "Startling Orange" mixed with three Farrow & Ball colors—"Cream," warm brown "Wainscot" and "India Yellow." Collections of handmade treasures, including Sicilian cake molds and a primitive zinc cow's head, add to the room's celebration of handcraftsmanship and design.

On the second floor, nine bedrooms were designed for the constant use of visitors. One of the most popular is the striking hot pink and orange suite, whose bright colors are a pleasant surprise in the classic mansion. Embroidered bed linens in a cheerful sixties palette set the theme and are highlighted by the golden glow of walls covered in raffia. Exotic accents such as the Middle Eastern inlaid bone and amber mirror over the bed add to the room's appeal.

The Venetian bedroom is much quieter, a serene mélange of underwater blues and grotto greens, warmed by the chartreuse panels of Scalamandré silk that drape the canopied bed. A comfortable, skirted chair of Barry's design set by the fireplace is a favorite spot to read while gazing out at the bucolic countryside.

It is this blending of styles that is the key, Barry explains, for an inviting and personal space. Building on his home's traditional Edwardian architecture, he supplemented it with his own designs and antiques, creating a new and welcoming aesthetic for the gracious old country manor.

A collection of ninety-two framed Victorian shadowboxes of seashells make a striking wall unit. Comfortable furnishings include a channel-backed leather wing chair and vintage red Chesterfield sofa, *left*. ▪ The book-lined library is centered on a "Nettie Darr" table, one of Barry's first designs for Mike Reid Weeks and inspired by his grandmother's parlor table. Tall Lucite floor lamps provide light at either end of the oak daybed, *above*. ▪ An octagonal turret expands the end of the library and is set for scholarly pursuits with antique globes, a Victorian drafting table and comfortable leather seating. Cozy plaid panels of Brunschwig & Fils "Ombre Stripe" twill across the windows highlight the views of the fields and forests, *facing*.

OVERLEAF: The family room is warm and inviting in a harvest palette of golden raffia-covered walls and ceiling painted with Farrow & Ball "India Yellow." Centered on the classical fireplace, which is original to the room, furnishings are an eclectic mix of Barry's designs, such as his "Zeus" ottoman, "Barrymore" skirted chair and mementoes of his travels.

A corner banquette in the butler's pantry is a convenient place for breakfast and light meals. Morris "Apple" wallpaper continues from the kitchen on the walls, its informal, country charm being the perfect complement to the willow table from Anthropologie, *above left*. ▪ An antique street lamp from Paris hangs over the oak worktable inspired by Lutyens' Castle Drogo kitchen in southwest England. A Viking range nestles into the space where a fireplace used to be and is topped with a concave custom steel hood, *above right*. ▪ Storybook illustrations from Maxfield Parrish inspired the design of a handcrafted cabinet along one wall for plates and dishes. Poured concrete counters, tile-covered walls and Arts and Crafts oak cabinetry blend harmoniously with the rolling fields seen through the window, *facing*.

The second-floor hall stretches the length of the home and its architecture is celebrated with Farrow & Ball "Old White" paint. A translucent wire mesh pedestal designed by Barry supports a Carrera marble bust found in Sicily, *above left*. ▪ The Venetian bedroom looks out over the rolling front lawns. Walls are painted misty blue "Borrowed Light" from Farrow & Ball, which complements the chartreuse Scalamandré silk curtains on the canopied bed. Original oak floors are left uncovered, *below left*. ▪ Another guest bedroom glows in a sixties' palette of hot pink and orange—a pleasant update for the room's classically arched and diamond-paned window. The mesh bedside tables were designed by Barry with mirrored tops to complement the mirrored table across the room, *facing*.

Barry's Tips

- When making a formal room less so remember to keep it true to its origins; keep architectural elements such as molding and trim and preserve the original footprint.

- Translucent, linen scrims are a simple way to partition a space adding mystery and romance without permanent changes.

- Update a favorite heirloom for a personal look—the glass balls and claw feet from Barry's grandmother's parlor table were transferred onto a modern, wire mesh version in his library.

- Use natural colors that stimulate the appetite in the kitchen—the hues of the sun, wheat in the outdoor fields, vegetables in the garden.

- A bright color on the ceiling adds warmth—both the music and family room ceilings were painted strong yellow making them sunny and inviting.

RESOURCES

ANTIQUES

Amy Perlin • www.amyperlinantiques.com
Antiques on 5 • www.antiqueson5.1stdibs.com
David Bell • Tel: 202.965.2355
DHS Designs • dhsdesigns@aol.com
E. J. Grant • www.grantantiques.com
Gore-Dean • www.goredean.com
Ed Hardy • www.edhardysf.com
Hastenings • Tel: 540.687.5664
J. F. Chen • www.jfchen.com
Kenny Ball Antiques •
    www.kennyballantiques.com
Miller and Arney • www.millerarney.com
Neal Johnson Ltd. • NealJ@perigee.net
Randall Tysinger • www.randalltysinger.com
Stephane Olivier • www.stephaneolivier.fr
Susquehanna •
    www.susquehannaantiques.com

ARTISANS

Agora Interiors • Tel: 703.823.7800
Architectural Ceramics •
    www.architecturalceramics.net
Avery Fine Art • www.averyart.com
Carol Studios • Tel: 703.204.2050
Halgren O'Brien • Tel: 540.341.7527
Kelly Metalworks • Tel: 301.854.4848
Konst Construction • www.konstlifestyle.com
Mitchell Yanosky • www.mitchellyanosky.com
Old Town Woodworking • Tel: 540.347.3993
Portfolio Kitchens •
    www.portfoliokitchens.com
Renaissance Tile •
    www.renaissancetileandbath.com
Warnock Studios • Tel: 202.537.0134
Waterworks • www.waterworks.com

CARPETS

AMS Imports Inc. • www.amsimports.com
Elizabeth Eakins • www.elizabetheakins.com
Floor Gallery • www.thefloorgallery.com
Megerian • www.megerianrugs.com
Odegard • www.odegardinc.com
Stark • www.starkcarpet.com
Timothy Paul • www.timothypaulcarpets.com

FABRICS

Bennison • www.bennisonfabrics.com
Bergamo • www.bergamofabrics.com
Brunschwig and Fils • www.brunschwig.com
China Seas • www.quadrillefabrics.com
Clarence House • www.clarencehouse.com
Cowtan and Tout • www.cowtan.com
Donghia • www.donghia.com
Elitis • Tel: 703.465.5512
Fortuny • www.fortuny.com
Gisbert Rentmeister • Tel: 202.646.1774
Henry Calvin • www.henrycalvin.com
Hodsoll McKenzie • Tel: 800.996.9607
Jasper • www.johnrosselli.com
Kathryn Ireland • www.kathrynireland.com
Larsen • www.cowtan.com
Lee Jofa • www.leejofa.com
Lulu DK • www.luludk.com
Manuel Canovas • www.manuelcanovas.com
Morris and Co. • www.william-morris.co.uk
Myung Jin • www.myungjinfabric.com
Old World Weavers • www.fonthill-ltd.com
Osborne and Little •
    www.osborneandlittle.com
Peter Fasano • www.peterfasano.com
Pierre Frey • www.pierrefrey.com
Pollack • www.pollackassociates.com
Quadrille • www.quadrillefabrics.com
Raoul Textiles • www.raoultextiles.com
Robert Kime • www.robertkime.com
Rogers and Goffigon • Tel: 203.532.8068
S. Harris • www.sharris.com
Sanderson • www.sanderson-uk.com
Scalamandré • www.scalamandre.com
Schumacher and Co. • www.fschumacher.com
Sea Cloth • www.seacloth.com
Sister Parish • www.sisterparishdesign.com
Stroheim & Romann • www.stroheim.com
Tyler Graphics • Tel: 202.319.1100
Vervain • www.vervain.com
Watts of Westminster •
    www.wattsofwestminster.com
Zimmer and Rhode •
    www.zimmer-rhode.com
Zoffany • www.zoffany.com

FURNITURE LINES

Amy Howard •
    www.amyhowardcollection.com
Baker • www.bakerfurniture.com
Christian Liaigre • www.christian-liaigre.fr
David Iatesta • www.davidiatesta.com
Dennis and Leen • Tel: 310.652.0855
Formations • Tel: 310.659.3062
George Smith • www.georgesmith.com
Hickory Chair • www.hickorychair.com
Ironies • www.ironies.com
Janus et Cie • www.janusetcie.com
Julia Gray • www.juliagraymindwire.com
Lewis Mittman/Edward Ferrell • www.
    lewismittman.com
McGuire • www.mcguirefurniture.com
Michael Taylor www.michaeltaylordesigns.com
Mike Reid Weeks • Tel: 843.851.6968
New Classics • www.newclassics.biz
Niermann Weeks •
    www.niermannweeks.com
O. Henry House • www.ohenryhouseltd.com
Oly • www.olystudio.com
Panache • www.panachedesigns.com
Patina • www.patinainc.com
Pierce Martin • www.piercemartin.com
R. Jones • www.rjones.com
Rose Tarlow—Melrose House •
    www.rosetarlow.com
Stone Yard • www.stoneyardinc.com
Sutherland • www.sutherlandteak.com
Tomlinson/Erwin-Lambeth •
    www.tomlinsonerwinlambeth.com
William Switzer •
    www.williamswitzercollection.com

SHOWROOMS

Ainsworth Noah • www.ainsworth-noah.com
At Home Nashville •
    www.athomenashville.com
Donghia • www.donghia.com
Hinc • www.hincshowroom.com
Hines and Co. • Tel: 202.484.8200
Hinson and Co. • Tel: 202.646.0260
Holly Hunt • www.hollyhunt.com
J. Lambeth • www.jlambeth.com
John Rosselli •
    www.johnroselliantiques.com
The Martin Group •
    www.martingroupinc.com
Michael Cleary • Tel: 202.488.9787
Patricia Group • www.patriciagroup.com
Smith Grubbs • www.smithgrubbs.com